SMART-OPEDIA

Maple Tree Press Inc.
51 Front Street East, Suite 200, Toronto, Ontario M5E 1B3
www.mapletreepress.com

Maple Tree Press Edition © 2007

© 2003 Éditions Nathan/VUEF, Paris, France for the first edition
© 2005 Éditions Nathan, Paris, France for the current edition
Original edition: DOKÉO 6–9 ANS.

Distributed in Canada by Raincoast Books
9050 Shaughnessy Street, Vancouver, British Columbia V6P 6E5

Distributed in the United States by Publishers Group West
1700 Fourth Street, Berkeley, California 94710

Cataloguing in Publication Data

Smart-opedia : the amazing book about everything / Eve Drobot, translator.

Includes index.

Original French title: Dokéo.

ISBN 13: 978-1-897349-03-8 (bound) / ISBN 10: 1-897349-03-3 (bound)
ISBN 13: 978-1-897349-09-0 (pbk.) / ISBN 10: 1-897349-09-2 (pbk.)

1. Children's encyclopedias and dictionaries. 2. Encyclopedias and
dictionaries. I. Drobot, Eve, 1951-

AG6.S62 2007   j031   C2007-901699-5

AUTHORS

Chapter openers:	Anne Bleuzen
	Didier Lévy
Astronomy:	Nathalie Audard
The Earth:	Philippe Monges
Plants:	Philippe Monges
Animals:	Frédéric Denhez
The Human Body:	Maryline Coquidé
History:	Dimitri Casali
Today's World:	Julien Hirsinger
The Arts:	Sylvie Baussier
Science and Technology:	Joël Lebeaume
Text for North American edition:	Eve Drobot

ILLUSTRATORS

Cover:	Clément Oubrerie
Chapter openers:	Gaëtan Dorémus
Know-It-All News:	Blexbolex
Astronomy:	Alexios Tjoyas
The Earth:	Charles Dutertre
Plants:	Vincent Mathy
Animals:	Marc Boutavant
The Human Body:	Nicolas Hubesch
History:	Pascal Baltzer
Today's World:	Arno
	Benjamin Bachelier
	Olivier Latyk
	Jörg Mühle
	Sandra Poirot-Cherif
	Fabrice Turrier
The Arts:	Aurélie Guillerey
Science and Technology:	Sylvie Bessard
Additional art for North American edition:	Claudia Dávila

We acknowledge the financial support of
the Canada Council for the Arts, the Ontario
Arts Council, the Government of Canada
through the Book Publishing Industry
Development Program (BPIDP), and the
Government of Ontario through the Ontario Media Development
Corporation's Book Initiative for our publishing activities.

ONTARIO ARTS COUNCIL
CONSEIL DES ARTS DE L'ONTARIO

Printed in China

A   B   C   D   E   F

SMART-OPEDIA

THE AMAZING BOOK ABOUT EVERYTHING

MAPLE
TREE
PRESS

CONTENTS

Amazing World!

Live It Up!

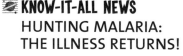

Then and Now

Genius at Work!

Introduction

If your brain is full of questions, then *Smart-opedia* has the answers! Expect to be fascinated and prepare to grow your smarts at each turn of the page.

With subjects so inviting and accessible, you can open at any page that catches your attention or read your way through from start to finish. Along the way, you'll make connections as you move from theme to theme, and you'll gather all sorts of knowledge that will help you to decipher the world around you, stay abreast of current events, and form an opinion on important issues.

Look out for these special features throughout:

FOOD FOR THOUGHT
Chapter introduction pages that offer myths, legends, famous quotes, and historical facts to give a broader perspective on the subjects that follow.

CAREER
Become familiar with diverse and sometimes unusual occupations, such as vulcanologists, air monitors, and architects.

KIDS' QUESTIONS + ANSWERS

A question-and-answer format answers questions you may not even know you had. For example: How many stars are there in the sky? Why do some animal parents abandon their young? Who makes weapons?

TIMELINES

See how we got from then to now: when Marco Polo arrived in China, when the pharaoh Cheops built the tallest pyramid, and when the Gameboy was invented in Japan.

Timeline

Spotlight on...

SPOTLIGHT ON...

Meet significant historical figures, such as Leonardo da Vinci, Anne Frank, Walt Disney, Mozart, and Alfred Nobel.

tune in

TUNE IN

Take a more in-depth look at a certain subject of interest.

Number Crunch

NUMBER CRUNCH

Get the statistical lowdown on everything from the temperature at the Earth's core to the number of cells in our brain.

KNOW-IT-ALL NEWS

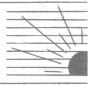

KNOW-IT-ALL NEWS

Special news features that focus on amazing subjects, such as the discovery of new medicines from plants, uncovering fossils in ice, child labor, the history of the circus, and the invention of the modern robot.

Hint: look out for the way that color codes link art and words on a page.

EVEREST

Amazing World!

According to the ancient Greeks and Romans, each constellation, or group of stars, tells a story. Three big stars in a row aren't just three big stars—they are the belt of a mighty hunter named Orion, the son of the sea god Poseidon. Orion was in love with Artemis, the goddess of the hunt, but her brother Apollo, the god of the sun, didn't approve. Apollo tricked Artemis into killing Orion. Heartbroken, Artemis sent Orion to shine from above.

Throughout history, people have been terrified by eclipses. In Vietnam, they believed that a huge frog was attacking the Moon. The Hindus believed a dragon was eating the Sun. In South America, they said a jaguar ate it. So, people yelled and banged on drums to keep all these hungry animals away. Nowadays we understand the relationship between the Sun, Moon, and Earth and know what causes the Earth to be darkened by an eclipse.

Astronomy

Professor Jumblebeard and the scientists of the Astronomers' Club take off into space, riding a gigantic mortar shell shot out of a huge cannon, and land right smack in the Man in the Moon's eye. That's the beginning of the first science fiction film ever made, *A Trip to the Moon*, made in France in 1902. But it was on July 21, 1969, at 2:56 in the morning on the international atomic clock, that the first human, astronaut Neil Armstrong, actually stood on the Moon and said these famous words: "One small step for man, one giant leap for mankind."

"Twinkle, twinkle, little star,
How I wonder what you are!
Up above the world so high,
Like a diamond in the sky."
Traditional nursery rhyme

On a summer night, you stare at the starry sky. You wonder: what is a star anyway? How many stars are there? How does Earth fit in? You're not the only one who has ever asked these questions. Over the years we've learned some of the answers, but there are still many more questions...

On October 30, 1938, the American radio network CBS interrupted its program for a live report: "The Martians have landed!" People in New York, Philadelphia, and Chicago panicked, and thousands packed the roads fleeing the invaders. The panic was real, but the report was not. It was actor Orson Welles performing his radio play *The War of the Worlds*, based on a famous science fiction novel by H.G. Wells.

13

The Solar System

The planets **orbit** around the Sun: they go around it in the shape of ellipses, while they themselves rotate.

It is made up of a huge star, the Sun, and eight planets that go around it. The system includes millions of other little stars...

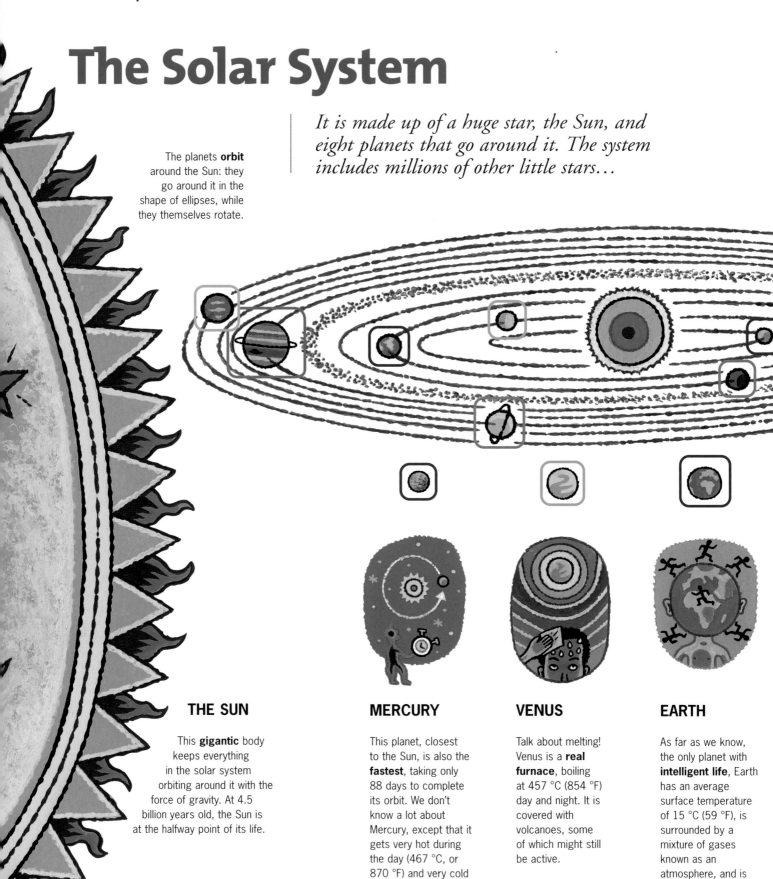

THE SUN

This **gigantic** body keeps everything in the solar system orbiting around it with the force of gravity. At 4.5 billion years old, the Sun is at the halfway point of its life.

MERCURY

This planet, closest to the Sun, is also the **fastest**, taking only 88 days to complete its orbit. We don't know a lot about Mercury, except that it gets very hot during the day (467 °C, or 870 °F) and very cold at night (–183 °C, or –297 °F).

VENUS

Talk about melting! Venus is a **real furnace**, boiling at 457 °C (854 °F) day and night. It is covered with volcanoes, some of which might still be active.

EARTH

As far as we know, the only planet with **intelligent life**, Earth has an average surface temperature of 15 °C (59 °F), is surrounded by a mixture of gases known as an atmosphere, and is largely covered by water.

Four planets—Mercury, Venus, Earth, and Mars—have a hard and rocky surface. The other four planets—Jupiter, Saturn, Uranus, and Neptune—are gigantic balls of gas without any real surface, with rings made of rocks, ice, and dust particles. The solar system also contains asteroids and comets. Asteroids are big rocks, and there are many of them forming a chain belt between Mars and Jupiter. Comets are made of dust and ice, and also circle the Sun in long and narrow ellipses.

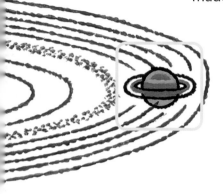

tune in

Planet No More

In 1930, Clyde Tombaugh discovered a ninth planet. An 11-year-old girl named Venetia Burney named it Pluto, after the Roman god of the Underworld, because it was dark and mysterious. In 2006, the International Astronomical Union voted to demote Pluto from planet to dwarf-planet status. The scientists decided Pluto was not big enough, not round enough, and too close to Neptune. Turns out Pluto had a lot of fans, and they were quite upset when their favorite planet got downgraded.

MARS

The **red** planet gets its color because of all the iron in the rocks that cover its surface. Underneath, there's a lot of ice, and possibly water. Mars has a huge volcano, Mount Olympus, which is 27 km (17 miles) high.

JUPITER

The **largest** planet. You'd need more time to go around Jupiter than you would to go from Earth to the Moon. On its surface is a giant red spot; it's an ancient cyclone, a swirling mass of gas that's like a hurricane. At its widest point, the spot is three times as big as Earth.

SATURN

Saturn's **rings** were first noticed in 1610 by the astronomer Galileo. There are thousands of them, and each ring is relatively very thin. One that has a diameter of 250,000 km (155,347 miles) or more is only 1.5 km (1 mile) thick.

URANUS

It goes around the Sun practically **lying down** while the other planets—apart from Venus, which is completely on its side—are only slightly inclined. It takes 42 years for the poles to alternate between light and darkness.

NEPTUNE

The **blue** planet was named after the Roman god of the sea. Neptune gets its color from methane, one of the gases in its atmosphere. It's also the windiest planet after Saturn, with gusts up to 2,000 km (1,245 miles) per hour.

To the Moon!

Four times smaller than Earth, the Moon is the only celestial body ever visited by humans. Will we live on it one day? We can only wonder...

Earth and the Moon are a happy pair, with the Moon 380,000 km (236,120 miles) away, turning tirelessly around Earth. They couldn't look more different: Earth is a blue marble full of life, the Moon looks gray and deserted. Yet our planet and its satellite have a common history. By studying Moon rocks, we can learn a great deal about the formation of Earth.

THE BEGINNING

About 4.5 billion years ago, baby Earth collided with another planet the size of Mars. **Earth and Moon** as we know them today were formed from that collision.

ROUND AND ROUND

The **Moon orbits Earth** about every 28 days. But because the Moon also spins on its own axis every 28 days, we always see the same face of the Moon from Earth.

MIGHTY MOON

The Moon is 400 times smaller than the Sun, but it is also 400 times closer to Earth. So the Moon can come between the Sun and the Earth and block out all the light. We call this a **solar eclipse**.

SO LONG?

The Moon gets **farther away from Earth** by 3 cm (1 1/4 in.) each year. Three billion years ago, it was one-third closer to us. If the Moon keeps moving like this, one day there will be no more solar eclipses.

From the Moon, Earth looks like a **blue marble**, thanks to its oceans. Between 1969 and 1972, 12 American astronauts walked on the Moon. The first one was Neil Armstrong.

We could also build an **"astroport"** on the Moon. Because the Moon has only one-sixth the gravitational pull of Earth, a rocket would take off from there much more easily.

The Moon doesn't have an atmosphere. That's why it makes a perfect **astronomical observatory**: there aren't any atmospheric disturbances like the ones on Earth.

The Moon is **very hot** (120°C, or 248°F) by day, and **very cold** (-180° C, or -292° F) at night.

The Moon's **landscape** consists of vast plains that are called "seas," deep craters, and mountains. The highest mountain is 8,200 m (26,900 ft.). The lunar surface is made up of rocks and dust.

The Moon's landscape is eroded only extremely slowly by wind or water. As a result, the **footprints** made by visiting astronauts are still there!

Because there's no atmosphere, meteors can crash onto the Moon and leave **craters** behind. The dust this stirs up settles very, very slowly.

Earth's atmosphere filters out harmful solar and cosmic rays. But on the Moon, you would have to wear a special space suit and seek shelter **underground**.

On Earth, air carries sound. Because the Moon has no air, **human voices** can't be heard.

The Stars and the Universe

With a simple telescope, or even just your eyes, you can see lots of things in the sky and start to understand what the universe is made of.

The universe was born 13.7 billion years ago out of a gigantic explosion called the Big Bang. Ever since, the universe has kept expanding. It started off very hot, but has cooled off bit by bit, and has produced the stars, grouped into galaxies, the planets, and other celestial bodies, which are then grouped into star clusters. As astronomers search the sky, they see that the universe continues to grow. But they still don't really know its future: will it stay the way it is, or will it eventually shrivel up and collapse in on itself?

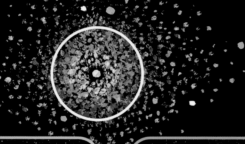

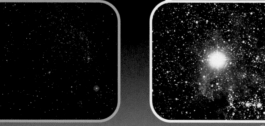

Looking at the night sky, the ancient Greeks and Romans grouped stars together and called them "constellations." Within the constellation called **Ursa Major, or Great Bear**, the seven brightest stars look like a spoon, and are known as the **Big Dipper**.

Stars are not all white. Their **color** depends on their surface temperature. The Sun's temperature of 6,500 °C (11,732 °F) makes it appear yellow. The hottest stars, with temperatures of more than 30,000 °C (54,030 °F), look blue.

The stars are born, live, and die. The biggest stars have a short life span and die quickly, in a violent explosion. They are called **supernovas.** The Sun isn't as big, and will probably explode in about 4.5 billion years. Then it will shrink as it slowly dies.

In this picture, all the stars seem to be spinning around the **Pole Star,** which looks quite still. In fact, we're the ones going around! And if the Pole Star looks like it's not moving, that's because it is aligned with Earth's rotational axis. It is rotating too.

How many stars are there in the sky?

You can see about 6,000 stars with your naked eye. But there are many, many more. Our galaxy alone consists of 100 billion stars, and there are 100 billion galaxies that have just as many. It's almost impossible to imagine how big the universe really is!

Stars produce their own light, but planets merely reflect the light of the star that shines on them. That's why the planets only shine at night. Some planets, like **Venus** (also called the Evening Star) are very bright, while others, like Uranus and Neptune, are barely visible.

When a **comet** goes near the Sun, its body of ice and dust melts enough to throw off a brilliant tail. Some comets have a regular orbit: Halley's comet passes between Earth and the Sun every 75 or 76 years. It was last seen from Earth in 1986 and will next appear in 2061 or 2062.

Some giant stars, when they die, create something almost unbelievable: a **black hole**. Black holes are so dense they swallow anything that comes near them. Nothing escapes a black hole—neither matter nor light. They are simply invisible. Scientists think there is a black hole in every galaxy.

A whole lot of stars together form a galaxy. Galaxies come in all shapes and sizes. The pretty white swirl of stars that you can see on a summer's night is the **Milky Way**, the galaxy to which our solar system belongs.

Space Trips

Human ingenuity finds better and better ways to explore space.

Since 1957, thousands of **rockets** have shot off into space, propelling shuttles and satellites. They are built in sections, or "stages" that fall off, and can only be used once.

From Earth

Optical telescopes use mirrors to capture light from celestial objects. They are usually built at high altitudes, where pollution and atmospheric interference are less likely. This Very Large Telescope (VLT) is in Chile.

Radio telescopes are huge antennas that can pick up sound waves from space. This Very Large Array (VLA), in New Mexico, is made up of 27 curved dish antennas.

Astronomers working in observatories use computers to analyze the information they receive from telescopes and satellites.

Why try so hard?

Because we're curious. Scientists want to understand how the universe came to be, what it's made of, and what will happen to it. We have a need to discover.

To contact other life forms. In 1977, we sent a message to extra-terrestrials on the Voyager. No one has answered. The Search for Extra-Terrestrial Intelligence (SETI), an international radio monitoring program, continues to listen to the skies.

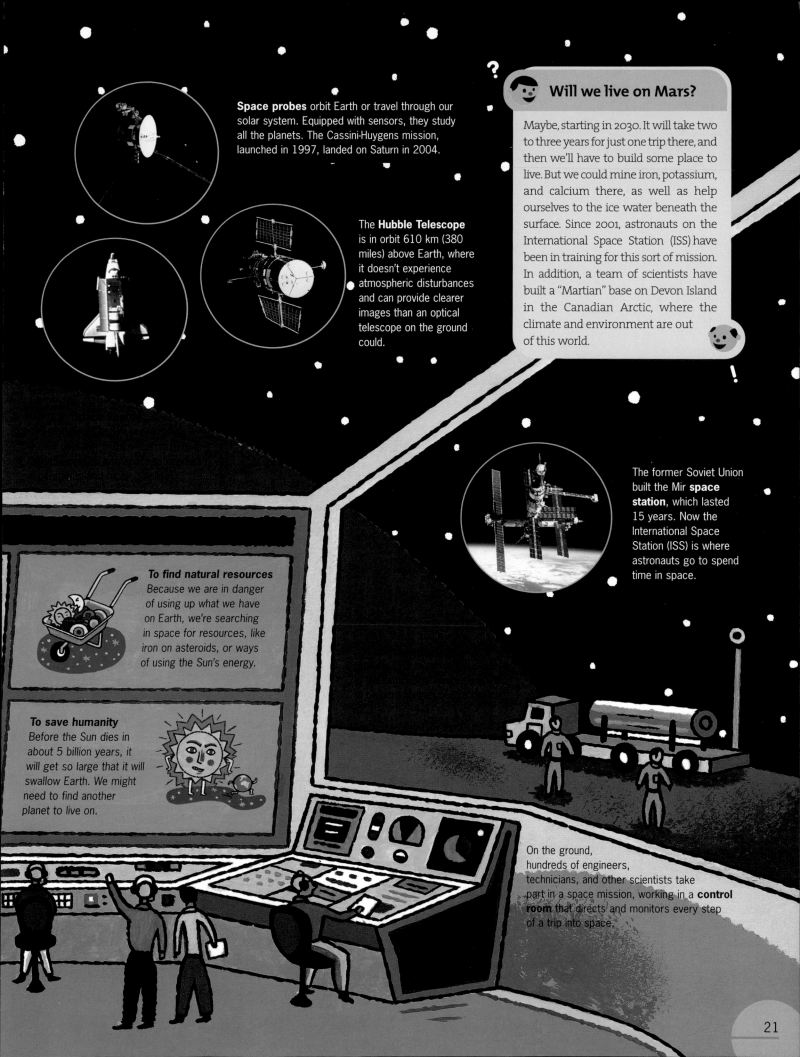

Space probes orbit Earth or travel through our solar system. Equipped with sensors, they study all the planets. The Cassini-Huygens mission, launched in 1997, landed on Saturn in 2004.

The **Hubble Telescope** is in orbit 610 km (380 miles) above Earth, where it doesn't experience atmospheric disturbances and can provide clearer images than an optical telescope on the ground could.

Will we live on Mars?

Maybe, starting in 2030. It will take two to three years for just one trip there, and then we'll have to build some place to live. But we could mine iron, potassium, and calcium there, as well as help ourselves to the ice water beneath the surface. Since 2001, astronauts on the International Space Station (ISS) have been in training for this sort of mission. In addition, a team of scientists have built a "Martian" base on Devon Island in the Canadian Arctic, where the climate and environment are out of this world.

The former Soviet Union built the Mir **space station**, which lasted 15 years. Now the International Space Station (ISS) is where astronauts go to spend time in space.

To find natural resources
Because we are in danger of using up what we have on Earth, we're searching in space for resources, like iron on asteroids, or ways of using the Sun's energy.

To save humanity
Before the Sun dies in about 5 billion years, it will get so large that it will swallow Earth. We might need to find another planet to live on.

On the ground, hundreds of engineers, technicians, and other scientists take part in a space mission, working in a **control room** that directs and monitors every step of a trip into space.

KNOW-IT-ALL NEWS

Vera Smart
Editor-in-chief

Ashley Asks
Interviewer

Tex A. Snap
Photo Journalist

Claire Itty
Researcher

Art Phul
Illustrator

Ed Shorter
News Briefs

From the Editor's Desk

The International Space Station (ISS) weighs more than 400 tonnes (440 tons) and orbits 400 km (248 miles) above Earth. Sixteen countries—including the U.S., Russia, France, Japan, and Canada—helped put it together.

Aboard the ISS

Teams of astronauts from all over the world spend months at a time on the ISS as an "expedition." In 2007, the crew was Expedition 15. Here's a peek at what their life is like aboard the ISS.

Aboard the Station, astronauts are still regular people: they eat, sleep, have to use the washroom.... But due to weightlessness, they drink their daily 3 litres (3 quarts) of water with a straw, and need to strap themselves to the bed when they go to sleep.

Vera Smart

Art Phul

Ashley Asks

Marco Hermann is a doctor with the European Space Agency (ESA).

How do you become an astronaut?
You have to pass tests given by NASA (National Aeronautics and Space Administration) and ESA. In the past, only armed forces members could apply. Now civilians are welcome. You need to be a highly qualified scientist, with good technical and medical knowledge, be in excellent physical and mental health, and have good team spirit. And it helps if you're not claustrophobic!

How long do astronauts have to train?

Apprentice astronauts take five years of practical and technical courses, in addition to physical training. There are survival training exercises held in the woods and at sea. And there are sessions in a pool and on motion simulators to train for weightlessness. Virtual reality simulators are used as well, to give a feel for life on the Station.

SPACE GEAR
THE RIGHT THING FOR THAT LONG SPACE TRIP!

Guaranteed air and heat !!!

Tex A. Snap

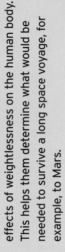

In their laboratory-cabins, astronauts work on experiments that can't be done on Earth, and try out new materials and medicines. One thing they study, for instance, is the effects of weightlessness on the human body. This helps them determine what would be needed to survive a long space voyage, for example, to Mars.

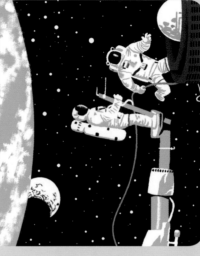

Weightlessness is not kind to human beings! It takes a lot of getting used to. At first, astronauts suffer from space sickness. And they need to work out on stationary bikes for at least two hours a day to keep their muscles, including the heart, from atrophying.

Attached to the station by cables, astronauts do repairs in space. Their pressurized suits provide breathing air, keep them warm, and protect them from harmful rays. But it's not easy to loosen a bolt when you're weightless!

Ed Shorter

News Briefs

Astrotourism

In 2001, an American businessman named Dennis Tito became the first tourist in space. He paid 20 million dollars to spend a week aboard the ISS, being careful not to get in the astronauts' way.

Send popcorn!

The ISS is restocked with supplies by unmanned spacecraft, such as the Russian *Progress*, which are sent from Earth and radio-controlled. They bring fuel, replacement pieces, equipment, scientific materials, and food and water for the astronauts. The astronauts themselves travel to and from the ISS on the Space Shuttle.

Ed Shorter

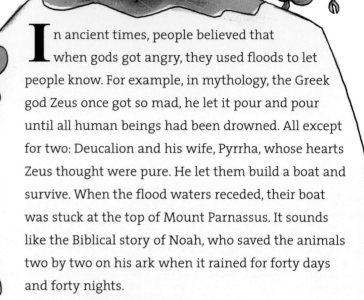

> "Those who dwell among the beauties and mysteries of the Earth are never alone or weary of life."
>
> Rachel Carson, 1907–1964

In ancient times, people believed that when gods got angry, they used floods to let people know. For example, in mythology, the Greek god Zeus once got so mad, he let it pour and pour until all human beings had been drowned. All except for two: Deucalion and his wife, Pyrrha, whose hearts Zeus thought were pure. He let them build a boat and survive. When the flood waters receded, their boat was stuck at the top of Mount Parnassus. It sounds like the Biblical story of Noah, who saved the animals two by two on his ark when it rained for forty days and forty nights.

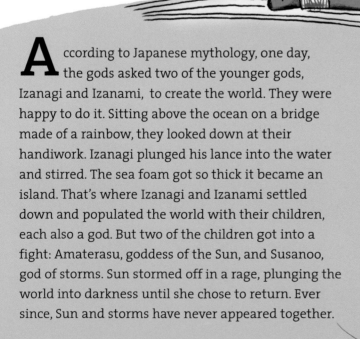

According to Japanese mythology, one day, the gods asked two of the younger gods, Izanagi and Izanami, to create the world. They were happy to do it. Sitting above the ocean on a bridge made of a rainbow, they looked down at their handiwork. Izanagi plunged his lance into the water and stirred. The sea foam got so thick it became an island. That's where Izanagi and Izanami settled down and populated the world with their children, each also a god. But two of the children got into a fight: Amaterasu, goddess of the Sun, and Susanoo, god of storms. Sun stormed off in a rage, plunging the world into darkness until she chose to return. Ever since, Sun and storms have never appeared together.

The Earth

According to another Greek myth, the goddess of wheat, Demeter, had a daughter named Persephone, who was kidnapped by Hades, god of the underworld. Demeter, crazed with grief, finally found her beloved daughter. She struck a deal with Hades: they would share Persephone, each having her for six months. When she was with her mother, it would be spring and summer, and the wheat would sprout and grow. But when Persephone went below Earth with Hades, autumn would arrive, and the wheat stalks would wither and die. And that's why we have seasons.

Mexican legend tells the story that Popocatepetl and Iztaccihuatl loved each other. But Izta's father wanted her to marry the bravest warrior in battle. So Popocatepetl went off to fight. When Izta heard a rumor that he'd been killed in the war, she died of a broken heart. But Popocatepetl came back, and he built two immense pyramids. On top of one, he laid Itza's body, and he himself sat at the top of the other, watching over her with a torch in his hand. Snow fell and covered the two lovers, but Popocatepetl's flame burned bright. That's the story of Iztaccihuatl and Popocatepetl, two of Mexico's famous volcanoes.

Earth has always been a mystery to us. Over thousands of years, we've explored our planet inside and out, and have learned a great many of its secrets. But Earth still blasts us with hurricanes and earthquakes. Could it be a reminder for us to always respect our planet?

25

Our World

Today we know that our planet is a large, rocky ball. We used to think that Earth was flat; we have spent centuries getting to know its every prairie, mountain, and sea, uncovering its mysteries.

4th century BCE	4th century BCE	1275, 14th century	1492	1522	1909, 1911
Alexander the Great's army reached India.	**Pytheas**, a Greek sea captain, sailed as far as England.	**Marco Polo** got to China by land, **Arab navigators** by sea.	**Christopher Columbus** crossed the Atlantic Ocean and landed in America.	**Magellan's** ship sailed around the world. Yes, the Earth *is* round!	American Robert **Peary** reached the North Pole; Norwegian Roald **Amundsen**, the South Pole.

This **strange 11th century map** is supposed to be of the Mediterranean region. Early maps were not precise, and were partly drawn from imagination.

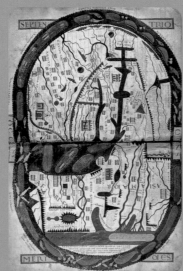

People thought **sea monsters** lived in the most far-off oceans.

Our ancestors

believed the Earth was flat. They were afraid that if they traveled too far, they would risk falling off the edge. Six hundred years ago, the Greek thinker Pythagoras figured out that the world was round, but no one listened to his idea. It wasn't until the 16th century that ships sailed around the world and proved his theory. Bit by bit, we've explored just about the world's entire surface.

Today, there are no large unknown territories left for us to discover. But all sorts of new methods and means of transport allow us to know our planet better and to explore the most inaccessible places: the remote polar caps, the hottest deserts, the highest mountains, and the densest tropical forests.

Satellites allow us to observe our planet from space.

No, there are still remote areas that have no contact with the modern world. It could be a part of the Amazon rainforest, a tiny island, a patch of desert.... Some are uninhabited, some are lived in by small groups of people who have adapted to life in the most difficult conditions. These places still hold mysteries to solve, and there are millions of plants and animals left to discover.

A **helicopter** can land in hard-to-reach areas.

Mountain climbers can reach the highest summits.

High in the treetops, scientists study the animals that live up in the rainforest canopy.

A **motor boat, canoe,** or **raft** can be launched for river or lake expeditions.

On **research ships,** scientists study the seas and oceans.

Divers can learn about marine life: coral, fish, shells, a whole universe of plants and animals....

In the 1960s, for the first time, **photos taken by satellites** allowed us to see what our planet looks like from space.

Submarines can descend 12 km (7 ½ miles) to explore the ocean floor.

27

All Around the Sun

Our planet is a big ball that flies through space at 100,000 km (62,140 miles) per hour, and circles the Sun in 365 days. It also rotates every 24 hours.

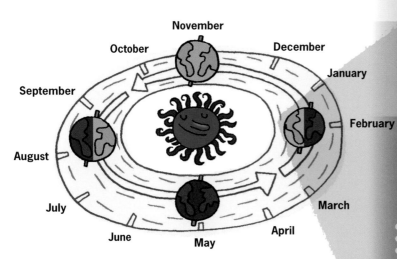

November

October   December

September   January

February

August

July   March

June   May   April

It's **winter** in the northern hemisphere, which is too far from the Sun to get much heat and light.

It's daytime on the west coast of North America; it's **3:00 p.m.**

Earth tilts by 23.5 degrees along its vertical axis—and that's why we have seasons. The North and South don't get the same heat from the Sun's rays at the same time. In February, it's winter in the North and summer in the South, which is tilted towards the Sun. In August, it's the opposite: halfway though its rotation around the Sun, it is summer in the North, which is turned towards the Sun, and winter in the South.

When it's day on one side, it's night on the other. When it's winter on top, it's summer on bottom. And vice versa...

The equator gets the same amount of Sun all year—there is **only one season**: hot and humid.

February in the Southern Hemisphere

The Sun's rays hit the South full on: it's summer.

February in the Northern Hemisphere

In the North, the rays are at an angle: it's winter.

It's summer in the southern hemisphere, which leans towards the Sun and gets a lot of heat and light.

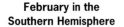

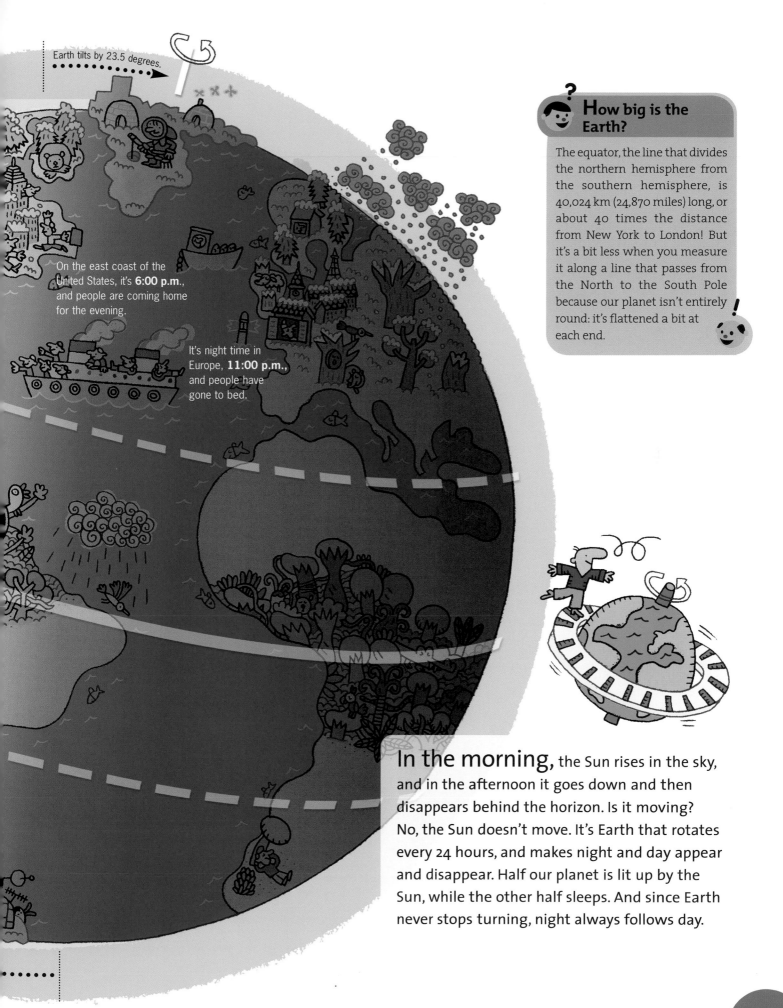

Earth tilts by 23.5 degrees.

On the east coast of the United States, it's **6:00 p.m.**, and people are coming home for the evening.

It's night time in Europe, **11:00 p.m.**, and people have gone to bed.

How big is the Earth?

The equator, the line that divides the northern hemisphere from the southern hemisphere, is 40,024 km (24,870 miles) long, or about 40 times the distance from New York to London! But it's a bit less when you measure it along a line that passes from the North to the South Pole because our planet isn't entirely round: it's flattened a bit at each end.

In the morning, the Sun rises in the sky, and in the afternoon it goes down and then disappears behind the horizon. Is it moving? No, the Sun doesn't move. It's Earth that rotates every 24 hours, and makes night and day appear and disappear. Half our planet is lit up by the Sun, while the other half sleeps. And since Earth never stops turning, night always follows day.

A Planet of Rocks and Fire

Mount St. Helen's, on the west coast of the U.S., spits up a gigantic, boiling hot **cloud of ash.**

Our planet is alive! It bubbles and bounces and spits lava and smoke from volcanoes. Let's explore Earth's crust in search of rocks, oceans, and continents...

Small, rounded mountains were once large, pointy ones that have been worn down by wind and rain.

Earth's surface doesn't keep still. The crust is made up of several plates. At Earth's core, fiery rocks boil over and move the plates away from or closer to each other. It's only a few centimetres a year, but over long periods, these separations or shocks create rifts, mountains, and volcanoes.

The **mantle** is made up of very hot fluid rocks that are always moving.

When plates collide, **volcanoes** are created. Fissures in the plates let the liquid rocks from beneath the crust escape as lava.

Number Crunch

4 km (2 ½ miles) is as far down below the Earth's surface people have ever gone. It happened in a mine in South Africa.

13 km (8 miles) is the deepest hole ever dug into Earth's crust, by drilling in Russia.

6,000°C (10,832 °F) is the temperature at Earth's core.

The crust, hard and rocky, is the outer "skin" of our planet. Earth's crust is thicker under the continents (35 km, or 22 miles) than it is under the oceans (5 km, or 3 miles).

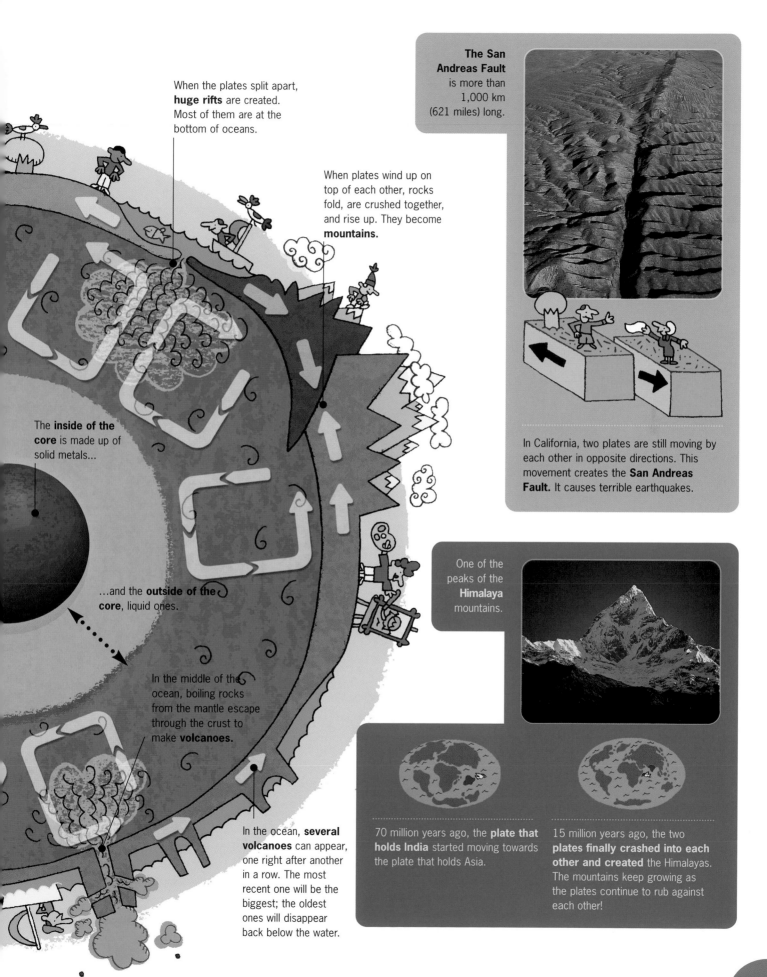

When the plates split apart, **huge rifts** are created. Most of them are at the bottom of oceans.

When plates wind up on top of each other, rocks fold, are crushed together, and rise up. They become **mountains.**

The **inside of the core** is made up of solid metals...

...and the **outside of the core,** liquid ones.

In the middle of the ocean, boiling rocks from the mantle escape through the crust to make **volcanoes.**

In the ocean, **several volcanoes** can appear, one right after another in a row. The most recent one will be the biggest; the oldest ones will disappear back below the water.

The San Andreas Fault is more than 1,000 km (621 miles) long.

In California, two plates are still moving by each other in opposite directions. This movement creates the **San Andreas Fault.** It causes terrible earthquakes.

One of the peaks of the **Himalaya** mountains.

70 million years ago, the **plate that holds India** started moving towards the plate that holds Asia.

15 million years ago, the two **plates finally crashed into each other and created** the Himalayas. The mountains keep growing as the plates continue to rub against each other!

KNOW-IT-ALL NEWS

Vera Smart
Editor-in-chief

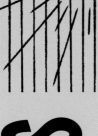

Ashley Asks
Interviewer

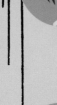

Tex A. Snap
Photo Journalist

Claire Itty
Researcher

Art Phul
Illustrator

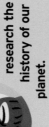

Ed Shorter
News Briefs

From the Editor's Desk

Antarctica is a large island that covers the South Pole. It doesn't belong to anyone. It is an international natural reserve dedicated to peace and science. Researchers of all nations live there for part of the year.

Vera Smart

Art Phul

Antarctica: Land of Science

Tex A. Snap traveled to the South Pole and visited the Amundsen-Scott Research Base, where 150 scientists live and study. It's a miniature city, with its own restaurants, movie theater, and hospital.

7:00 a.m. The winter sun is already shining brightly. Jeannie and Norbert meet for a big breakfast to build up their strength. It's -15 °C (5 °F) outside.

8:00 a.m. Jeannie and Norbert leave the base to watch the emperor penguins. Penguins are funny birds that can't fly, but swim as well as fish do.

Penguins going fishing.

Ashley Asks

Daniel Gelet is a scientist who is digging into the ice to research the history of our planet.

What are you looking for in the ice?
Air bubbles. We're walking on snow that has fallen and accumulated over hundreds of millions of years! If you dig deep down, you find very old air bubbles.

What do these bubbles tell you?
The air bubbles can tell us what the atmosphere was like a long time ago. We can figure out what the weather was like, and what Earth's

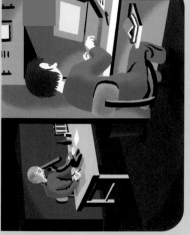

climate was before Neanderthal man came along.

More than 500,000 years ago?

Yes, when people hunted with wooden clubs and rocks. We have found climates that were much colder than today. Northern Europe was covered in glaciers, and the Sahara was not a desert. Many plants grew there, and there were lots of animals, like giraffes and elephants.

3:00 p.m. Norbert studies blood samples he took from the penguins. Jeannie checks her findings with other researchers around the world.

11:00 a.m. Penguins are not at all afraid. That's lucky for the researchers who are studying how these creatures survive in the cold.

Map

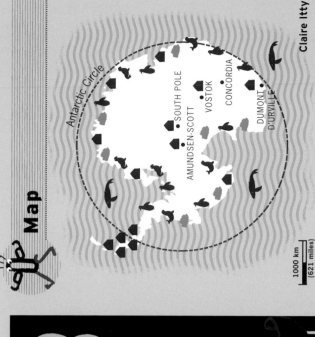
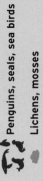

Antarctic Circle

SOUTH POLE
AMUNDSEN-SCOTT
VOSTOK
CONCORDIA
DUMONT D'URVILLE

1000 km
(621 miles)

Animals and plants are concentrated on the coasts where it is less cold than inland.

Penguins, seals, sea birds

Lichens, mosses

Research bases

Claire Itty

8:00 p.m. Researchers get together to compare notes. Jeannie is there, as well as Adelaide, who is studying the atmosphere. Bashir is there—he's visiting the research base to star gaze in the clear sky. And there's Daniel, who is studying the ice to discover historical climates.

Tex A. Snap

News Briefs

Sea lions were contaminated by a chicken virus. It's a reminder to all visitors not to leave any trash outside.

Record winds and temperatures blew in over the winter. Blizzards blew at 300 km (185 miles) per hour and the thermometer went down to -90 °C (-130 °F).

Extreme endurance athletes from around the world participate in the annual **Antarctic Ice Marathon**. Snow and ice are guaranteed for this chilly footrace.

Ed Shorter

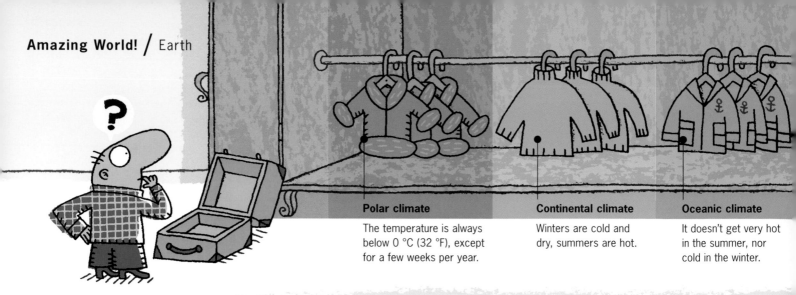

Polar climate
The temperature is always below 0 °C (32 °F), except for a few weeks per year.

Continental climate
Winters are cold and dry, summers are hot.

Oceanic climate
It doesn't get very hot in the summer, nor cold in the winter.

Earth's Many Climates

Hot, cold, windy, dry, or rainy. Weather changes depending on where you are in the world.

The continental climate has four **seasons**: spring, summer, fall, and winter.

In Asia, it rains for several months each year. This is the **monsoon season.**

The state of **California** and the coasts of Australia both have a **Mediterranean** climate.

Climate is the weather you have in one part of the world all year long. The local climate determines the local species of plants and animals, what kinds of people live there, what they eat, and what they wear. There are eight climates found around the world, but their boundaries aren't exact. Within the state of California, for instance, there are several different climate types—from desert to mountain—but most of the state has a Mediterranean climate, with cool rainy winters and dry summers.

tune in

How can the ocean make it both rain and shine?

New York, in the northeastern U.S., and Porto, on Portugal's west coast, are on the same latitude, which means that they are the same distance from the Equator. Yet, in the winter, New York always gets snow and Porto never does. That's because a cold ocean current cools New York, and a warm ocean current heats up Porto.

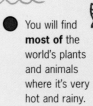

You will find **most of** the world's plants and animals where it's very hot and rainy.

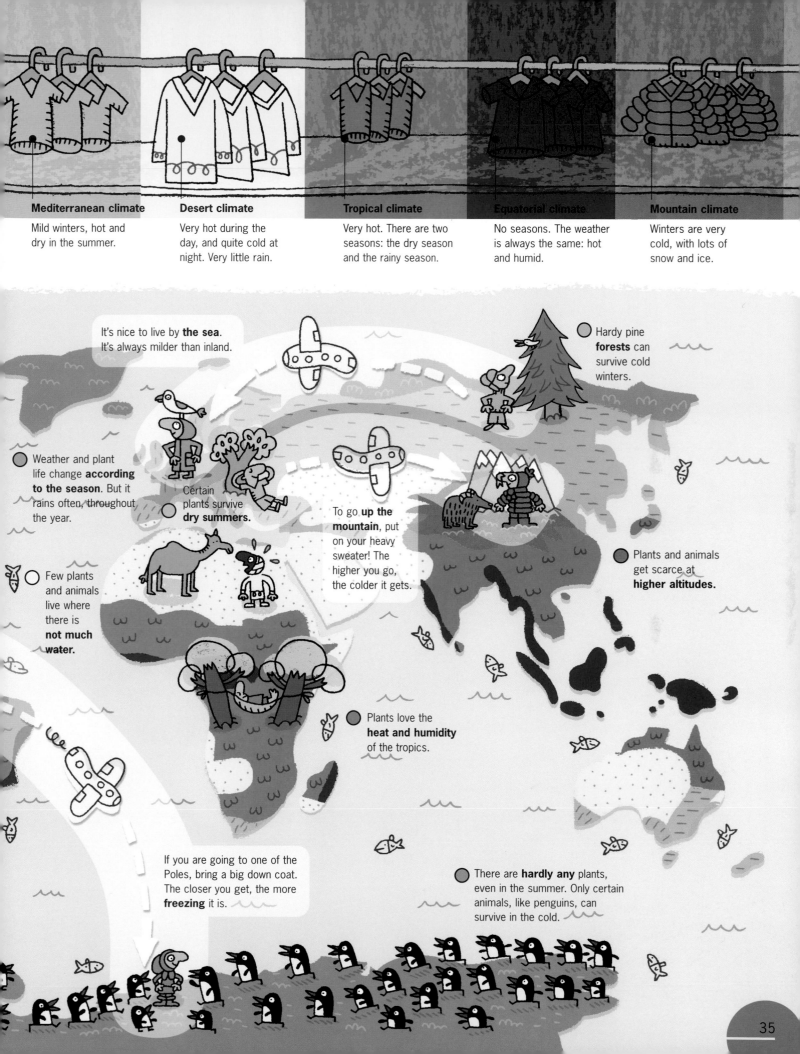

Mediterranean climate

Mild winters, hot and dry in the summer.

Desert climate

Very hot during the day, and quite cold at night. Very little rain.

Tropical climate

Very hot. There are two seasons: the dry season and the rainy season.

Equatorial climate

No seasons. The weather is always the same: hot and humid.

Mountain climate

Winters are very cold, with lots of snow and ice.

It's nice to live by **the sea**. It's always milder than inland.

Hardy pine **forests** can survive cold winters.

Weather and plant life change **according to the season**. But it rains often, throughout the year.

Certain plants survive **dry summers**.

To go **up the mountain**, put on your heavy sweater! The higher you go, the colder it gets.

Plants and animals get scarce at **higher altitudes**.

Few plants and animals live where there is **not much water**.

Plants love the **heat and humidity** of the tropics.

If you are going to one of the Poles, bring a big down coat. The closer you get, the more **freezing** it is.

There are **hardly any** plants, even in the summer. Only certain animals, like penguins, can survive in the cold.

A World of Difference

Here are two regions with totally different climates: the Sahara Desert, in Africa, and the Amazon Rainforest, in South America.

In the desert you'll find sand dunes, vast stretches of rocks, mountains, and oases. It's very hot and rarely rains. And yet, things manage to live there. Plants rely on night time humidity, and dig deep with their roots to find water. Animals go out at night and sleep all day to take shelter from the Sun.

Dunes are little mountains of sand that are shaped by the wind.

An **oasis** is a source of water, either at the surface or far below ground. Plants grow well there.

Antelopes are one of the few larger animals that can survive the desert heat.

Snakes lift their bellies to avoid getting burned by the hot ground.

Nomadic peoples cross the desert on camels and sleep in tents they carry.

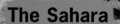

The Sahara

- **Size:** Takes up 1/4 of the African continent.
- **What is it?** The largest hot desert in the world.
- **Temperature:** Above 50 °C (122 °F) in the summer.
- **Rain:** Very few storms each year.

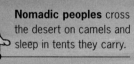

Just the smallest amount of rain will turn these little bushes green. Most of the time they are **yellow and dry.**

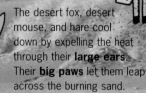

The desert fox, desert mouse, and hare cool down by expelling the heat through their **large ears.** Their **big paws** let them leap across the burning sand.

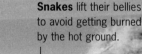

During the day, the **scorpion** hides out beneath rocks or under the sand.

Single tall trees, more than 70 m (230 ft.) high, rise up above the forest. Predatory birds live in their top branches.

70 m (230 ft.)

50 m (165 ft.)

Amazon Rainforest

- **Size:** Takes up 2/5 of the South American continent.
- **What is it?** Home of the most powerful river system in the world.
- **Temperatures:** 25 to 28 °C (77 to 82 °F) all year.
- **Rain:** Heavy rain 200 days of the year.

The light-filled top of the forest is called the **canopy.** This is where most of the animals live.

20 m (65 ft.)

The **center of the forest** is a tangle of tree trunks, vines, and leaves.

Equatorial forests are warm and wet. They are full of life. These forests are home to the most diverse species of plants and animals in the world. Each "level" of forest has its own wildlife, best suited to the conditions in that part of the forest. Unfortunately, Earth is losing a lot of its equatorial forests as we cut down trees for the wood, or level them to create farmland.

10 m (35 ft.)

It's **very dark** at the foot of these giant trees. The plant life above is so dense that very little sunlight filters down to here.

0 m (0 ft.)

A Watery Planet

Of all the planets in our universe, Earth is the only one where life could develop. What is the secret of this miracle? Water! Water, water everywhere, in all its forms and states.

Vapor rises into the sky, where it condenses and becomes clouds. The wind **pushes** the clouds across great distances.

Dams create electricity.

The air we breathe is more or less moist: it contains water in its **gas state**, as vapor.

Three-quarters of the water that evaporates rains back on the oceans and seas. The rest waters the continents.

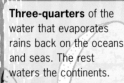

Water travels the Earth in many disguises. It's liquid in the sea, then becomes gas as it goes up into the sky; and it falls on mountaintops where it becomes ice. As it flows down the slopes, it is liquid again, creating rivers and streams that flow into the seas, back to where it started. On its journey, water nourishes living things. Human beings, and most animals and plants, are made up mostly of water. We need water all the time: to drink, to wash in, and to produce electricity. Water is precious!

Water in the sea, lakes, rivers, plants, and in the ground **evaporates into the air** when it is heated by the Sun.

Some of the rain that falls goes deep below the ground to form rivers and lakes known as **ground water.**

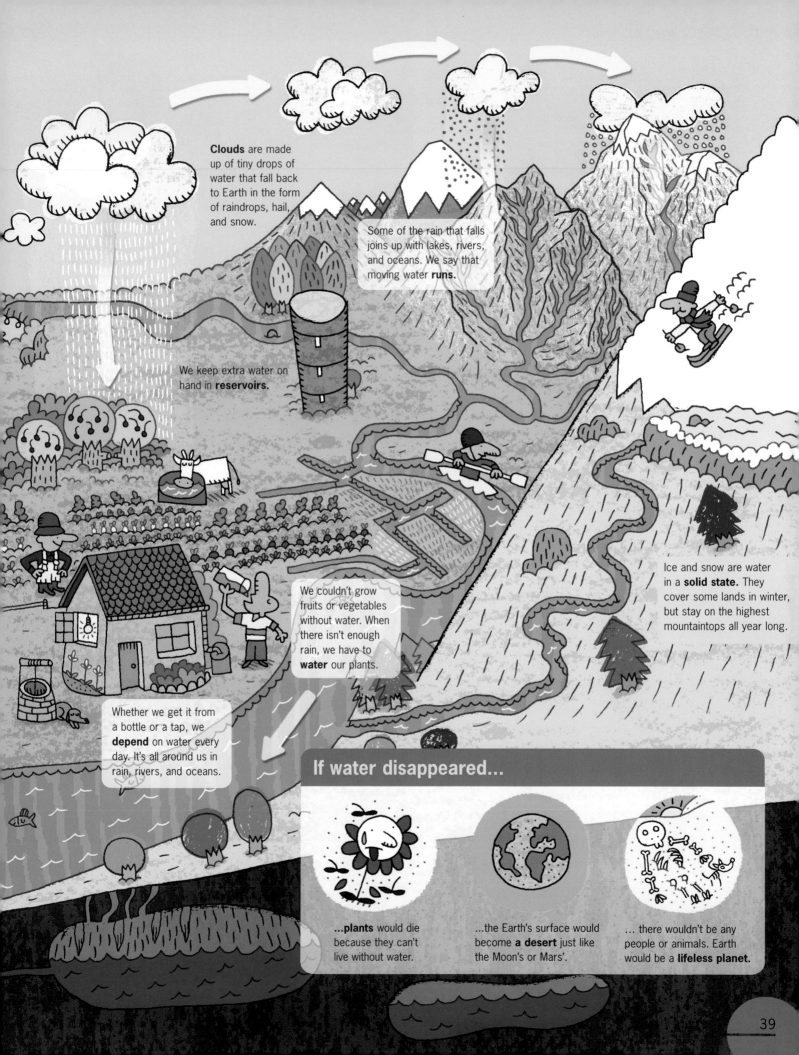

Clouds are made up of tiny drops of water that fall back to Earth in the form of raindrops, hail, and snow.

Some of the rain that falls joins up with lakes, rivers, and oceans. We say that moving water **runs.**

We keep extra water on hand in **reservoirs.**

We couldn't grow fruits or vegetables without water. When there isn't enough rain, we have to **water** our plants.

Ice and snow are water in a **solid state.** They cover some lands in winter, but stay on the highest mountaintops all year long.

Whether we get it from a bottle or a tap, we **depend** on water every day. It's all around us in rain, rivers, and oceans.

If water disappeared...

...plants would die because they can't live without water.

...the Earth's surface would become **a desert** just like the Moon's or Mars'.

... there wouldn't be any people or animals. Earth would be a **lifeless planet.**

The Ocean and Sea

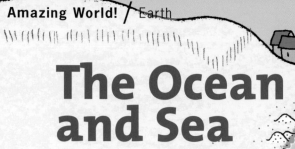

Seawater contains lots of salt. We collect it in **salt marshes** and use it to season our dinner!

Oil platforms bring up oil from beneath the ocean floor in huge pipes. They are built at the continental shelf, where the water is shallower.

You might have been to the beach, but you won't know the secrets of the ocean's depths unless you dive into the dark blue water...

Waves are created by the wind. Close to shore, they break and turn to foam.

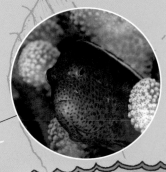

The descent closest to the shore is where you'll find the most **seaweed, coral, and fish.** This is where fish come to feed and reproduce.

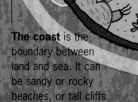

The coast is the boundary between land and sea. It can be sandy or rocky beaches, or tall cliffs.

Fish swim together in **schools** for protection.

The **continental shelf** is not far from shore. It's the last piece of land before a drop-off. It is rarely more than 200 m (655 ft.) deep.

The **continental embankment** looks like a huge underwater cliff. It is a steep slope into the abyss.

Record-Setting Seas and Oceans

- **The Arctic Ocean**, which covers the North Pole, is the coldest.

- **The Aral Sea** is almost dried out. Too much water is pumped out of the rivers that feed it.

- **The Atlantic Ocean** is crossed by the strongest ocean current, the Gulf Stream.

- **The Mediterranean Sea** is the world's largest sea.

- **The Dead Sea** is very salty. Nothing lives in it.

- **The Pacific Ocean** is the world's largest body of water.

NORTH AMERICA
EUROPE
ASIA
AFRICA
SOUTH AMERICA
Pacific Ocean
Atlantic Ocean
Indian Ocean

Seventy-one per cent of the Earth's surface is covered by water. Oceans are huge bodies that lie between continents. Seas are smaller, and have more coastlines. Millions of ships and boats cross the water in every direction: to fish, travel, and transport goods. Coastlines are heavily populated. You'll find the most living things—seaweed, coral, and fish—concentrated closest to shore. The bottom of the ocean is still waiting to be fully explored. The sea bed is a spectacular world of vast plains and dizzying depths.

Commercial ships carry 70% of the goods sold in the world. Oil tankers that clean out their holds in the open sea or, worse, have an accidental spill, leave tons of oil in the ocean.

A volcanic island is an underwater volcano that pops its head out above the water line.

Whales, dolphins, tuna, and other large sea animals travel great distances.

People can't breathe underwater. When they dive, they can breathe using air from **oxygen tanks.**

A **diving suit** is a stiff outfit pumped full of air that allows a person to go very deep.

A **submarine** is a ship that can travel underwater, even to the ocean floor.

Gas escapes from cone-shaped mountains in the **abyss.**

Parts of old **shipwrecks** at the bottom of the ocean offer fish shelter and protection.

A **ridge** is a mountain chain split by a crack. It is made by molten rocks escaping from inside the Earth.

As far down as 3,000 to 4,000 m (9,845 to 13,125 ft.), you will find living things, especially on the sides of volcanoes, where it's warm.

A **fault** appears when the ocean floor cracks open.

The **ocean floor** is very spread out, and sits 4 km (2 ½ miles) below the waterline.

The ocean's **abyss** is very deep! It can go down as far as 11 km (6 ¾ miles).

KNOW-IT-ALL NEWS

Vera Smart
Editor-in-chief

Ashley Asks
Interviewer

Tex A. Snap
Photo Journalist

Claire Itty
Researcher

Art Phul
Illustrator

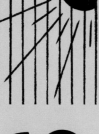

Ed Shorter
News Briefs

★ · ★ · ★ · ★ · ★

From the Editor's Desk

We don't know the full depths of the ocean very well yet—the abyss is so deep and hard to reach. Only a few very special submarines can explore these dark and mysterious spaces right now.

Voyage to the Sea Bottom

The *Nautilus* is a research submarine. It is lowered into the water from a ship and begins its scientific mission.

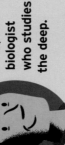

0 m / 0 ft.

Vera Smart

Art Phul

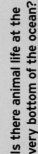
Ashley talks to Charles Tuba, a biologist who studies the deep.

Is there animal life at the very bottom of the ocean?
Yes, even thousands of metres down, there are tiny fish. They're all carnivores, meaning they eat other fish. There isn't any seaweed in their diet because down there it is too dark for any vegetation to grow.

What do they look like?
They often have huge eyes, which helps them see where there is practically no light. They also have big mouths full of teeth. They need all

There are three people aboard the *Nautilus:* the pilot and the co-pilot, who will steer the submarine, and a scientist, who will observe and choose specimens to collect from the sea floor.

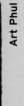

those teeth to be sure they don't miss out on any prey that goes by.

Do they spend all their time hunting?
No, actually, it's quite the opposite. These fish live in slow motion. Since they don't have much food, they need to conserve their energy. By moving slowly and only when they need to, they can survive even though food is scarce.

WANTED

HIDING IN THE OCEAN'S ABYSS

PLEASE SUPPLY ANY INFORMATION

THAT WILL HELP US FIND THEM

LET US KNOW!

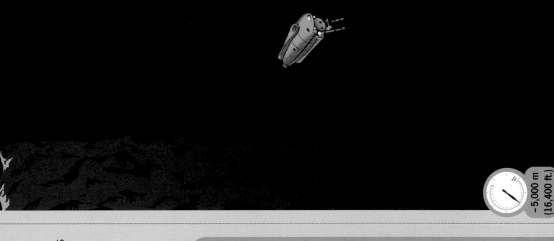

−4,000 m (13,120 ft.)

−5,000 m (16,400 ft.)

The submarine goes down into the abyss. It can descend to 6,000 m (19,685 ft.). Its powerful lamps light up the dark ocean floor.

−6,000 m (19,685 ft.)

The Nautilus samples gases that escape from the ocean floor. It also collects rocky deposits that could contain precious metals that we might mine one day.

0 m (0 ft.)

Mission accomplished! The submarine is lifted back onto its host ship by a team of experts. The samples the Nautilus brought back will now be studied. Bit by bit, we are discovering the ocean's secrets.

Tex A. Snap

The Scoop

Scuba divers explore underwater while breathing from a tank. The word "scuba" comes from **S**elf-**C**ontained **U**nderwater **B**reathing **A**pparatus. It takes training to learn how to do it, but it is a sport enjoyed by millions of people, as well as an aid to science.

News Briefs

Fishpeople

Researchers can study the oceans by scuba diving. But they can only go so deep because water pressure increases as you go down and is dangerous.

Precious Metals

There are very rich deposits of iron, nickel, and copper under the ocean floor. But extracting them is still too difficult and expensive. For now, we still mine these metals only on land.

Ed Shorter

Nothing But Air

Of all the planets in our solar system, Earth is the only one that has an atmosphere—a protective layer of air that allows us to live and grow. Let's take care of it!

The atmosphere is a mass of air covering the planet as high up as 700 km (435 miles) from Earth's surface. It is made up of 78% nitrogen, 21% oxygen, and the rest is carbon dioxide, hydrogen, methane, and ozone. The higher you go, the thinner the air is. The atmosphere regulates the temperature on the surface of our planet with the greenhouse effect. It also filters out dangerous ultraviolet rays. Without the atmosphere, we wouldn't exist!

Heterosphere

The last step before **space.** The air is too thin to breathe up here!

Meteorites are rocks that fly through space. They burn and are destroyed when entering our atmosphere.

Mesosphere

The mesosphere protects us from **meteorites.** We call them "shooting stars."

Ultraviolet rays can be deadly. Luckily, ozone gas in the stratosphere keeps them out of our air.

Stratosphere

At this level, **ozone** gas swallows up ultraviolet rays.

Troposphere

This is the lowest level of the atmosphere, where **clouds and rain are formed.**

It's because of **the atmosphere,** which regulates the surface temperature and filters out harmful rays, that humans, plants, and animals can live on Earth.

700 km
(435 miles)

−1,200 °C
(−2128 °F)

The layers... [text obscured] goes through... climbs back up again... considerably with the altitude.

Satellites orbit at between 400 and 1,500 km (250 and 930 miles) above Earth.

The space shuttle is on a mission 400 km (250 miles) above Earth.

80 km
(50 miles)

−90 °C
(−130 °F)

For hundreds of years we have been damaging the atmosphere. Our heating plants, factories, airplanes, boats, and cars spit out dangerous gases. The polluted air we breathe can cause serious illness. Some gases heighten the greenhouse effect, meaning Earth is growing warmer. Other gases, which used to be found in refrigerators and spray cans, have damaged a part of the ozone, which protects us from ultraviolet rays. People are becoming more aware of how our practices have taken a toll on the environment and are learning what we can all do to preserve the air we breathe.

48 km
(30 miles)

0 °C
(32 °F)

Weather balloons measure temperature 30 km (18 miles) above Earth.

16 km
(10 miles)

−56 °C
(-69 °F)

If the atmosphere disappeared…

Ultraviolet rays would kill humans, plants, and animals.

The average temperature would be **− 18 °C (under 0 °F)** because there'd be no greenhouse effect.

It would be **100 °C (212 °F)** during the day, and **− 150 °C (-238 °F)** at night.

Airplanes fly 12 km (7 ½ miles) above our heads.

Mount Everest, the world's tallest mountain, is 9 km (5 ½ miles) high.

Rice paddies and cows emit gases that contribute to global warming.

The atmosphere traps heat from the Sun, as a greenhouse would, and this warms up the air. That's why we call it the **greenhouse effect.**

Cars and factories pollute with carbon dioxide, which contributes to global warming in a major way.

Aerosol cans are safe now, but the gases they once used damaged the ozone.

Airplanes carry instruments to measure the weather.

Weather balloons carrying small radios fly up to 30 km (18 ½ miles) high and send back air temperature, humidity, and pressure level readings at different altitudes.

When enough tiny droplets of water vapor in the clouds stick to each other, they become raindrops. **Rain** falls because water is heavier than air.

Snow and hail are made in the clouds. The temperature needs to be 0 °C (32 °F) or lower, or they would melt.

Weather Station

Meteorological stations measure temperature, humidity and wind speed, as well as cloudiness, rain, and snowfall.

Hometown

Air in the atmosphere is warmed by the Sun and moves constantly. This is what causes **wind.**

There are **11,700 volunteer** weather watchers who report weather activity to the U.S. Weather Service.

The Weather

What a wind !

Force 0
Calm. No wind.

Force 2
Light breeze. Leaves rustle.

Force 4
Moderate wind. Curtains flap.

Force 7
Strong wind. Hard to walk into it.

Force 10
Gale. Trees are uprooted.

Force 12
Hurricane. Roofs are blown off and cars are tossed.

Rain, shine, wind? Modern technology is used to predict the weather. Here's a tour of a weather center.

Every morning, people pay attention to the weather report so that they know what to wear. That part is easy! But getting this information together is a lot of work. Hundreds of people collect and interpret thousands of bits of information observed on land, sea, and in the air. These measurements are analyzed by powerful computers that can perform 300 billion operations a second. The forecasters read the results and add their own experience and a bit of intuition. But don't ask them to forecast the weather for more than seven days ahead. Our atmosphere changes far too often to make that possible.

Satellites photograph the planet and clouds, and take the temperature of the oceans.

The **weather center** analyzes information that comes from all over. To be able to make forecasts for the next few hours or days, the center has to function 24 hours a day, every day.

Number Crunch

70 °C (158°F) is the highest temperature, reached in the Sahara.

-92 °C (-134 °F) is the lowest ever, measured in Antarctica.

320 km (199 miles) per hour is the strongest recorded wind, also in Antarctica.

1.87 m (6 ft.) is the most rain that has fallen in two days, on Reunion Island, in the Indian Ocean, in 1952.

The weather center issues **weather bulletins.** You can find them on the radio, on television, by telephone, and on the Internet.

If the weather is really bad, it's too dangerous for planes to take off and ships to sail. For many people, long range weather forecasts are vital. Others might find them useful to help them decide simple day-to-day things, like what to pack for a vacation.

Weather Center

Earth's Fury

When the ground shakes or volcanoes spit out boiling lava, and when wind and rain are whipped up, there's not much that can be done. It's not always possible to predict catastrophe.

There's no way to stop natural disasters. All we can do is stay ahead of the storm and floods, to flee from volcanic eruptions, and to take proper shelter when it's available. Many catastrophes are unpreventable. But there are others that are a result of human carelessness, like forest fires, mudslides, and some avalanches.

Cutting down trees and then building on a hillside weakens the soil. In places where it rains a lot, water can carry the earth away in the form of **mudslides.**

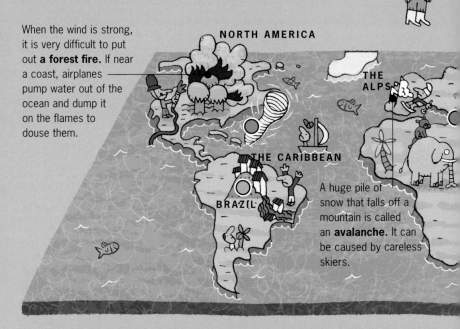

When the wind is strong, it is very difficult to put out **a forest fire.** If near a coast, airplanes pump water out of the ocean and dump it on the flames to douse them.

NORTH AMERICA

THE ALPS

THE CARIBBEAN

BRAZIL

A huge pile of snow that falls off a mountain is called an **avalanche.** It can be caused by careless skiers.

career

vulcanologist

Vulcanologists are scientists who study volcanoes. They watch them, film them, follow their history, and analyze their lava, gases, and rock formations. Vulcanologists try to find out what causes eruptions so they can predict when these strange mountains will spit fire again. With their help, people can be warned of danger.

In tropical regions, a warm air current rising from the warm sea can become a whirling wind called a **cyclone or a hurricane.** The incredibly powerful wind storm lifts everything in its path, including cars, trees, and houses.

A **tsunami** is a gigantic ocean wave caused by an underwater earth-quake. They are rare and usually occur in the Pacific Ocean. When it reaches land, a tsunami wave can be as high as 30 m (100 ft.).

Earthquakes can rip up a road, or bring a bridge or building tumbling down. We never know when one is going to start. In areas prone to earthquakes, houses are built to withstand them. Some of them are built on a foundation with special springs.

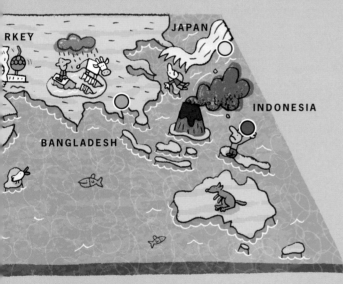

When there is a lot of rain or a run-off of snow from the mountains, rivers can overflow, and water suddenly rushes over land. These **floods** happen a lot in Asia during the monsoon season of heavy rains, and can cause great damage.

Volcanoes are sort of the steam valves of our planet: they let out molten rocks from inside the Earth's crust, and spit out lava, gases, and ash that cover the surrounding countryside. We try to keep an eye on volcanoes, but they erupt quickly and usually without advance warning.

Live It Up!

FINISH

Legend has it that long, long ago the trees were so tall they tickled the clouds. Kids would climb all the way up. You probably know the story of one—a boy named Jack who went up a magic beanstalk and made life miserable for the giant who lived there. Another traditional story tells that the inhabitants of the skies didn't like young visitors one bit, so they moved the sky upwards to where they couldn't be reached.

The fairy tale forest was full of strange goings-on. It's where Hansel and Gretel, left behind by their parents, met the witch who lived in a gingerbread house. It's where Merlin the Magician and Morgan la Fey worked their enchantments. It's where Little Red Riding Hood met the Wolf on her way to her grandmother's house. And it's where poor, lost Snow White found shelter at the house of the Seven Dwarves. Anything could happen in the woods!

Have you ever heard of a narcissus? It's a beautiful spring flower with white petals and a yellow trumpet. Do you know where it got its name? According to an ancient Greek myth, Narcissus was a beautiful young man, but he didn't know it because he had never looked in a mirror. Narcissus spent his time alone, walking through the woods. One day, tired after a long walk, he leaned over a clear pool of water to have a drink. There, he saw his reflection for the first time. He was so taken with his good looks that he stayed transfixed, staring at his own image. Narcissus stayed for so long that he took root on the banks of the pool and slowly turned into the flower that bears his name.

Plants

> "All plants are our brothers and sisters. They talk to us and if we listen we can hear them."

American Indian Proverb

Imagine a glorious garden, with majestic trees, bright flowers, and lovely fruit. There, the Bible tells, lived Adam and Eve, in the Garden of Eden. They lived without fear or shame. God had given them permission to eat all the fruit in the garden, except those on the Tree of Knowledge. One day, Eve met the serpent. He hissed at her to eat the Forbidden Fruit, which he said would make her God's equal. Eve gave in to his temptation, and then persuaded Adam to have a bite, too. God was furious! He threw them out of the Garden to live in the cruelty of the world. They lost their innocence, and the bounty of the Garden.

They can't move around, but they are definitely alive. Just like you, they breathe, eat, and grow. And like you they can adapt to their surroundings. Plants aren't just beautiful—they are essential to life. In fact, they take care of us!

Plant Families

*Thousands of plants grow on Earth.
We group similar ones into categories,
or "families." Let's take a walk...*

Mushrooms
No flowers, no roots—just a stalk with a cap. Mushrooms are fungi and come in many shapes, sizes, and colors. They grow quickly in humid places. They feed off other organisms, living or dead. Some are poisonous to humans.

Fungus grows on tree trunks.

Chanterelles and **porcinis** are delicious and safe to eat...

Parasol pine

Jack pine

Plants are living things. The smallest ones are too small to see, and the biggest ones are taller than a building. Some plants live in the water, others in the driest desert, and some on mountain tops. Scientists and nature lovers have counted over 32,000 different plant species in the world, from ordinary blades of grass to majestic trees, and from poisonous mushrooms to sweet-smelling flowers. There are four main groups of plants, divided by their characteristics: plants with flowers, plants without flowers, fungi, and conifers.

Cypress

Larch

Conifers
Trees that have fruit in the form of cones are called conifers. They have leaves shaped like needles and they don't lose them in autumn. They are also called resinous because they produce a sticky substance called resin. Conifers grow naturally in almost all parts of the world.

Fir

Algae
This plant doesn't have stems or roots. Algae live in water and humid places and need a lot of light. They can be red, brown, blue, or green.

Ferns
The littlest ferns are as big as your thumb, the largest are bigger than a house. They don't have flowers, but they do have lots and lots of leaves.

Moss
Moss is made up of many, many tiny stems all linked together. They like moist and dark places like the forest floor.

Plants without flowers

...but other mushrooms, like the **fly agaric** and the **death cap** are fatally poisonous. Never eat mushrooms you pick wild.

Crocus, iris, tulips, and daffodils... They all flower in spring.

The seed of an **oak** is called an acorn.

Grapes and pumpkins are fruits of **the vine.**

Plants with flowers
This group of plants includes all of the trees that lose their leaves in the autumn, as well as grasses, wheat, barley, and rice. All of these plants have some sort of flower. They reproduce by the seeds that are hidden in their fruit.

Water lilies float in ponds.

55

The Life of a Tree

It takes years for a tiny apple seed to become a tall and beautiful tree. Here is the story of an apple tree growing through the seasons.

Like all plants, trees are born, grow, reproduce, and die. In a temperate climate, the life of a tree is governed by the seasons. Each year, fruit trees produce flowers that become the fruit, which contains seeds. An apple tree produces hundreds of seeds, but only a few will become new trees.

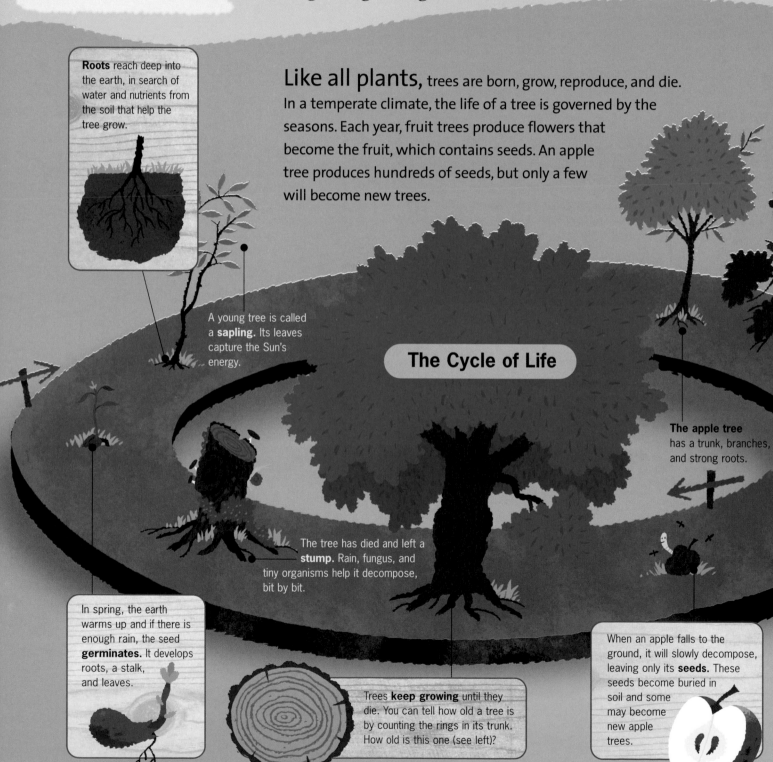

Roots reach deep into the earth, in search of water and nutrients from the soil that help the tree grow.

A young tree is called a **sapling.** Its leaves capture the Sun's energy.

The Cycle of Life

The apple tree has a trunk, branches, and strong roots.

The tree has died and left a **stump.** Rain, fungus, and tiny organisms help it decompose, bit by bit.

In spring, the earth warms up and if there is enough rain, the seed **germinates.** It develops roots, a stalk, and leaves.

Trees **keep growing** until they die. You can tell how old a tree is by counting the rings in its trunk. How old is this one (see left)?

When an apple falls to the ground, it will slowly decompose, leaving only its **seeds.** These seeds become buried in soil and some may become new apple trees.

56

It's winter.
The tree has no leaves. It's not dead, it's just resting. It will wake up when the warm weather returns in spring.

In the winter, a **bud** has a protective coat. It opens up in the spring to become a leaf or a flower, which in turn becomes a fruit.

Leaves fall in autumn. They fertilize the soil around the tree and help feed it in winter.

It's fall.
The last apples drop from the tree. The leaves dry out and turn red.

Insects drink nectar from the flowers. As they go from flower to flower, they carry pollen. Pollen helps the trees to grow new apples, and to reproduce.

The Seasonal Cycle

It's spring.
The apple tree is covered with leaves and flowers. Their color and scent attract insects.

It's summer.
The tree is loaded with apples. Depending on what kind of apple tree it is, its fruit will either stay green, or turn yellow or red.

Flowers on the apple tree turn into **fruit**. The fruit grows larger. It contains the seeds that make new apple trees.

57

Those Clever Plants

It's not easy being a plant in a world full of danger. Fortunately, plants have a few tricks tucked into their roots, their leaves, and their pretty flowers.

Plants have a lot of natural enemies. At any moment, they could be nibbled to bits by an insect or chewed up by herbivores. To survive, plants have some pretty amazing ways of defending themselves. They have also been able to adapt to harsh climates, like that of the desert. This adaptation took hundreds of thousands of years.

Yuckety-yuck...
The black-wood tree keeps antelopes from chewing it by having leaves that taste very bitter.

Call for back up...
When caterpillars go after cotton and corn, the plants emit an odor that attracts small wasps. The wasps attack the caterpillars and eat them up.

Set a trap...
The venus fly-trap is a hardy plant that manages to survive in poor soil by living on insects. It makes a delicious nectar that draws flies onto its leaves and then snaps shut and swallows them.

Stay warm...
Tulips spend the winter huddled inside their bulbs, which are buried in the ground. When spring comes, they grow again.

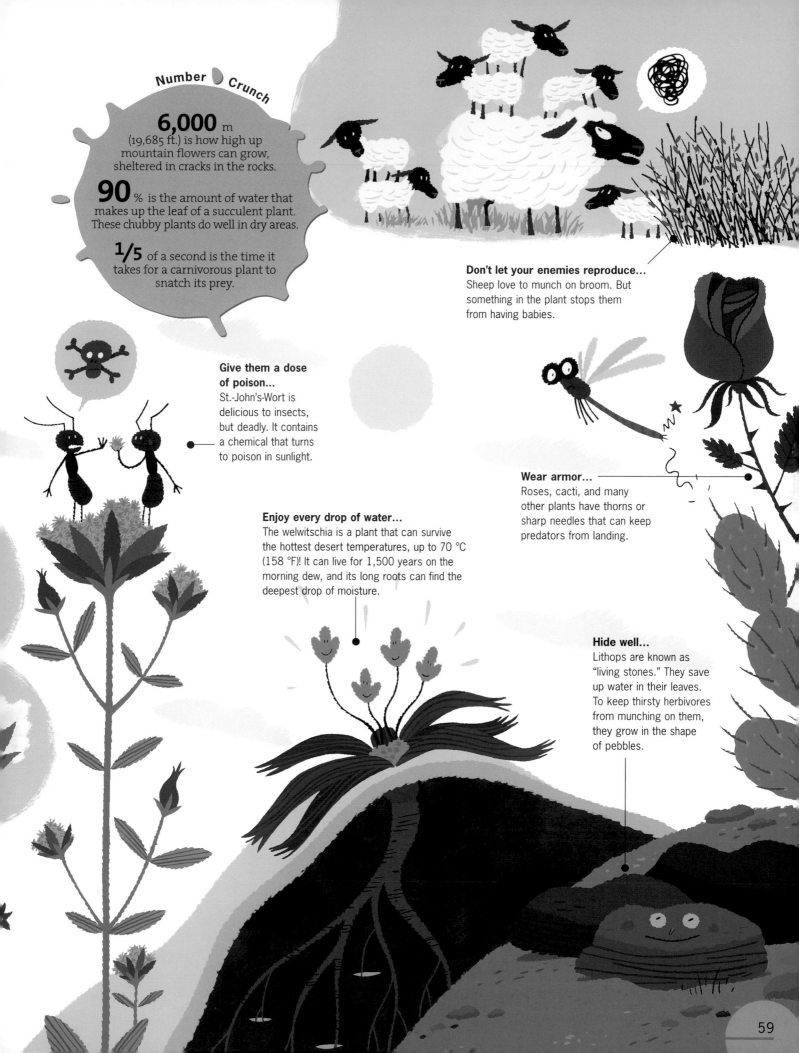

Number Crunch

6,000 m (19,685 ft.) is how high up mountain flowers can grow, sheltered in cracks in the rocks.

90 % is the amount of water that makes up the leaf of a succulent plant. These chubby plants do well in dry areas.

1/5 of a second is the time it takes for a carnivorous plant to snatch its prey.

Don't let your enemies reproduce...
Sheep love to munch on broom. But something in the plant stops them from having babies.

Give them a dose of poison...
St.-John's-Wort is delicious to insects, but deadly. It contains a chemical that turns to poison in sunlight.

Enjoy every drop of water...
The welwitschia is a plant that can survive the hottest desert temperatures, up to 70 °C (158 °F)! It can live for 1,500 years on the morning dew, and its long roots can find the deepest drop of moisture.

Wear armor...
Roses, cacti, and many other plants have thorns or sharp needles that can keep predators from landing.

Hide well...
Lithops are known as "living stones." They save up water in their leaves. To keep thirsty herbivores from munching on them, they grow in the shape of pebbles.

KNOW-IT-ALL NEWS

Vera Smart
Editor-in-chief

Ashley Asks
Interviewer

Tex A. Snap
Photo Journalist

Claire Itty
Researcher

Art Phul
Illustrator

Ed Shorter
News Briefs

Notes from the Editor's Desk

Without plants, life would not be possible. Not only do they feed us and give us materials for all sorts of objects and clothing, they also heal us. Sixty percent of the medicines we use come from plants.

Vera Smart

Art Phul

Amazing Plants Heal Us

Scientist Max Pilo travels around the world looking for plants. But why? To find new sources of medicines. Let's visit him in Madagascar.

For Tovo, the traditional healer in the village of Andranavo, the jungle is a complete pharmacy. Here he finds all sorts of plants and herbs that help heal the people of his village. Max observes and listens carefully. He knows he can learn a lot from Tovo.

Ashley Asks

Ashley spoke to Esther French, an ethno-botanist. Esther studies how plants are used by different people around the world.

How long have people been using plants?
Forever. Early humans started off by eating them (grains, fruit, herbs), then making arms and tools out of them (wood spears, digging sticks) as well as using them to make clothes and parts of their houses. Soon we learned to farm plants—the earliest forms of agriculture go back 10,000 years or more.

Are there still some people who use nothing but plants in their daily lives?
Not really. Even tribespeople in distant parts of the Amazon and the Pacific use modern manufactured goods, too.

Are plants still necessary to these people?
For sure. They live in much the same way as their ancestors lived—relying on nature for most of their food. And in remote areas, the jungle is the only drugstore nearby. They have learned over many generations how to use dozens of different plants as medicines.

A few weeks later, Max returns home with suitcases full of plant samples. He has carefully noted exactly where each plant grew. Once back in his lab, he will study them.

Tovo uses a cream from local plants to heal a villager's wound. He has also made a herbal tea for a woman with a stomach ache. To the villagers, the healer is their family doctor.

A few years ago, the extract from a periwinkle in Madagascar proved a useful weapon in the fight against cancer. Maybe Max's botanical research will result in a new medicine too.

Tex A. Snap

The plants are analyzed by powerful equipment that can reduce them to tiny molecules. Extracts are tested on animals, and then on human volunteers, to see whether they are effective against specific illnesses.

Words to Know

Molecules are the basic building blocks of life. Every living thing on Earth—plants, rocks, animals, and even humans—is made up of molecules.

A **pharmaceutical company** or **drug firm** is a business that makes and sells medicines.

News Briefs

Marine Life may become a source of new drugs. Teams of medical scientists have been studying marine life for years, and several kinds of coral, algae, and shellfish have already yielded medicines.

Alert! Plants are for everyone, say people opposed to drug firms patenting certain native plants and making a profit from them. These plants have been used by native healers for centuries. Pharmaceutical companies can't now say that they're the only ones with a right to use them.

Ed Shorter

FOOD FOR THOUGHT

"
When a man wants to kill a tiger, it's called sport. When a tiger wants to kill a man, it's called ferocity."

George Bernard Shaw (1856–1950)

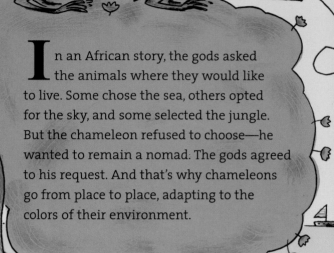

In an African story, the gods asked the animals where they would like to live. Some chose the sea, others opted for the sky, and some selected the jungle. But the chameleon refused to choose—he wanted to remain a nomad. The gods agreed to his request. And that's why chameleons go from place to place, adapting to the colors of their environment.

According to the Bible, God was very unhappy with the way people were acting and unleashed a flood to drown them all. Only Noah, his wife, their three sons, and their wives found grace in God's eyes. God ordered Noah to build an ark, and to fill it with animals, two of each species. Rain kept pouring down, and the ark sailed for 150 days until the waters retreated. The animals landed, and repopulated the Earth with their kind. Today, we see certain species are in danger of disappearing.

After a terrible shipwreck, an English aristocrat named Lord Greystroke, his wife, and their infant son washed up on the coast of Africa. The parents died, but the baby boy was adopted by Kala, a female gorilla, who brought him up among the great apes. This is the beginning of the story of *Tarzan, Lord of the Jungle*, written by Edgar Rice Burroughs in 1912.

Animals

Whether they have paws or claws, live in the water or up in the air, are all gray or multi-colored, are tiny or gigantic, animals are fascinating. They are all part of the life forms that appeared on this planet millions of years ago. Are we just another kind of animal?

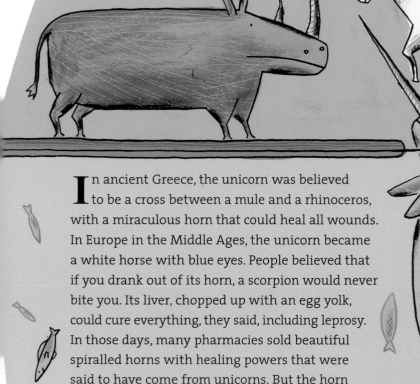

In ancient Greece, the unicorn was believed to be a cross between a mule and a rhinoceros, with a miraculous horn that could heal all wounds. In Europe in the Middle Ages, the unicorn became a white horse with blue eyes. People believed that if you drank out of its horn, a scorpion would never bite you. Its liver, chopped up with an egg yolk, could cure everything, they said, including leprosy. In those days, many pharmacies sold beautiful spiralled horns with healing powers that were said to have come from unicorns. But the horn really came from a narwhal, a kind of whale. That's because unicorns have never existed...except in people's imaginations!

The Dinosaurs

We continue to discover dinosaur fossils—remnants that help us understand these great extinct animals.

This is **Mongolia**, in the **Cretaceous period,** about 80 million years ago. The countryside is green and lush, with giant ferns and flowering plants.

In 1841, Richard Owen, an English paleontologist, came up with the word "dinosaur," which means "terrible lizard" in Greek. He used it to describe all the reptiles that lived in the Triassic, Jurassic, and Cretaceous periods of Earth's history, from 225 to 65 million years ago.

1 The collar on **Protoceratops** (whose name means "first horned face") served as a shield for males who fought each other.

2 Protoceratops was a small grass-eating dinosaur. It was only 1.8 m (6 ft.) long. It lived in herds near swamps.

1 Protoceratops' collar, bony growths on its jaws, and a beak like a parrot helped it defend itself against predators.

2 Protoceratops' teeth grew along a jaw that resembled scissors. They were used to grind up tough plants. If a tooth wore out, it would regrow.

3 Iguanodon footprints are usually found in groups, proving that the animals lived in herds. They also show this dinosaur moved slowly.

225 million years ago, many species of animals were wiped out when the climate began to shift. The one species that did survive was the reptiles, including dinosaurs. They lived all over the entire world and took on many forms. Some were the size of a chicken, others larger than elephants; there were herbivores and carnivores; fast ones and slow ones. We have discovered about 1,000 different kinds. Dinosaurs disappeared 65 million years ago, perhaps because of a meteorite crashing into Earth.

3 Iguanodon walked on all fours. Living in herds helped the adults protect the younger ones.

Iguanodon is one of the first dinosaurs ever discovered. Its teeth are similar to a modern iguana lizard, and Iguanodon is probably its ancestor.

4 It was long believed that **Oviraptor** (which means "egg thief") ate the eggs of other dinosaurs. But it ate the hard shells of its own.

5 Velociraptor (which means "fast thief"), ran quickly and hunted quietly. It grabbed its prey using its arms, and killed using its teeth and feet.

6 Tarbosaurus ("frightening lizard") was a cousin of the *T. rex*. It could weigh as much as 5,000 kg (11,025 lb.). It was too heavy to run, and probably had to eat other dinosaurs' kills.

4 Oviraptor laid its eggs in bunches, like today's sea birds. It looked like an ostrich and probably cared for its young.

5 Velociraptor's second toe had a very sharp claw that could cut like a razor blade.

6 Tarbosaurus's 15 cm (6 in.) long and piercing teeth could work through the toughest flesh of the biggest dinosaurs.

Gone But Not Forgotten!

Since the beginning of life on Earth, certain animals have disappeared forever. Or came very close....

QUETZALCOATLUS

This flying reptile of the **pterosaur** family had a wing span of 12 m (40 ft.). Without a doubt, it was the largest flying animal of all time. It became extinct at the same time as the dinosaurs.

A member of the **plesiosaur** family, this 15 m (49 ft.) long sea reptile was a fearsome predator in the days of the dinosaurs. It disappeared along with them.

The **thylacine, or Tasmanian tiger,** was exterminated on the mainland of Australia by dingoes 12,000 years ago. It survived on the island of Tasmania until the 20th century, when it was wiped out by sheep ranchers.

ELASMOSAURUS

TASMANIAN TIGER

In the millions of years that there has been life on Earth, many species have thrived and evolved. Some have disappeared, while their genetic cousins have adapted to become new forms of life. Many became extinct without leaving any descendants—but the disappearance of some dominant groups allowed others to take over. When the dinosaurs were gone, for instance, more kinds of mammals began to spread across our planet.

MAMMOTH

The last **quagga zebra** died in a zoo in 1893. It had disappeared from the wild in the 1880s. The zebra was wiped out by hunters who went after it for its skin and its meat.

QUAGGA ZEBRA

There have been **five great extinctions** in the animal kingdom. In each one, 60 to 96% of all species then alive disappeared. That was the case when the dinosaurs vanished. We don't really know what caused these extinctions. One possible explanation is climate change. These days there may be a sixth extinction underway, caused by human beings. As the rainforest is destroyed, dozens of invertebrate species are wiped out every second.

Next to Go?

Spix macaw
0 in the wild
(70 in captivity)

Mountain gorilla
Fewer than 750

Sumatran tiger
About 500

Mediterranean monk seal
About 500

PASSENGER PIGEON

Two hundred years ago, **passenger pigeons** traveled in flocks of hundreds of thousands. They were overhunted, and by 1914 they were all gone.

Different species of **mammoths** have roamed the Earth. The first ones lived 4 million years ago. The most recent ones, which are related to Asian elephants, survived until about 5,000 years ago.

DODO

The flightless **dodo** was an easy prey for hunters. The bird vanished from its home on the island of Mauritius in 1680.

DIATRYMA

The **diatryma** lived about 40 million years ago. It was 2 m (6 1/2 ft.) tall, but it didn't fly—it hunted, like a Velociraptor. Its giant claws and enormous beak were fearsome weapons.

The saber-toothed tiger was king of the North American plains 3 to 4 million years ago. It resembles the lion and tiger, both of which are its distant cousins.

After 500 million years in the sea, **ammonites** are gone the way of the dinosaurs. The octopus and the nautilus are distant descendents of these molluscs.

AMMONITE

SMILODON

Who's Who?

There are far too many animals for us to know them all. Currently, we know of 1.5 million different species. But there could still be millions more to discover.

Spider

Butterfly

Parrot

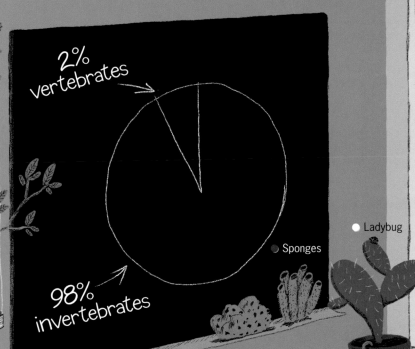

2%
vertebrates

98%
invertebrates

Sponges

Ladybug

Tick

Woodlouse

Earthworm

Mouse

Orangutan

Scorpion

Invertebrates

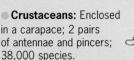

- **Insects:** Body in 3 parts; 3 sets of legs; 1 million species.

- **Arachnids:** 4 pairs of legs; 75,000 species.

- **Molluscs:** Soft body, often protected by a shell; 50,000 species.

- **Crustaceans:** Enclosed in a carapace; 2 pairs of antennae and pincers; 38,000 species.

- **Cnidarians:** Soft body, often has tentacles; 9,000 species.

- **Annelids:** Soft body, made up of rings; 14,000 species.

- **Echinoderms:** Body often covered in spines; 6,000 species.

- **Sponges:** The simplest multi-cell animals; 5,000 species.

- **Myriapods:** Body divided into segments, and lots of feet; 12,000 species.

Bee

Mussel

Shrimp

Millipede

Number Crunch

700 million
is how many years ago the first animals appeared.

235 is how many species of primate exist in the world. Humans are just one species.

150,000 kg (330,693 lb.) is the weight of a blue whale, the largest animal.

Vertebrates

■ Birds

Covered in feathers, birds' wings and their hollow bones allow most of them to fly. They use lungs to breathe and they feed themselves, using a beak without any teeth. They lay eggs. Over 9,600 species.

Owl

■ Reptiles

They can have no legs, or four legs. They can live on land or in water and use lungs to breathe. Most reptiles lay eggs. Their skin is covered with scales, or they have a shell. Group includes crocodiles, turtles, iguanas, dragons, snakes, and lizards. More than 6,900 species.

Turtle

Mammals

Most have four legs, except marine mammals, like seals or whales. They almost all have skin that is covered with hair. Most mammals give birth to fully formed babies, who are nursed by their mothers. They use lungs to breathe. Their internal temperature is constant, and that allows them to adapt to different climates. More than 4,600 known species.

Cow

■ Fish

They live in water, except for lungfish, which can live partly on land. Their skin is covered with scales, and they breathe through gills. Most of them lay eggs. There are cartilaginous fish (rays, sharks) and bony fish. 51,000 species.

Sea Horse

Trout

■ Amphibians

They live on land, but their babies live in water and breathe like fish. In fact, frogs, tritons, toads, and salamanders (4,800 species) always need water. They breathe with lungs, but also through their skin, which is wet and has no scales.

Salamander

Most animals move around. They eat, breathe oxygen, reproduce. Ever since the first animals appeared in the sea, the animal kingdom has continued to grow larger and more complex. These days, zoologists classify animal species into two groups: invertebrates, or those that don't have a skeleton, and vertebrates, or those that do.

Snail · Ant · ■ Angelfish ● Coral

● Grasshopper

● Stick insect

○ Fly

■ Shark

● Leech

■ Vulture · ■ Giraffe

■ Flamingo

● Sea anemone

○ Octopus

■ Iguana

○ Sea urchin

■ Orca

■ Cobra

● Cockroach

- Frog · ■ Toad

■ Hummingbird

○ Lobster

○ Starfish

■ Tiger · ■ Crocodile

■ Turtle

■ Beaver

Stay or Go?

For one reason or another, some animals always stay close to home, while others wander far and wide.

There are animals that run away

from winter and hunger. They migrate to warmer climates to find something to eat. Other animals are nomads, never staying in the same place, no matter what the season. There are others still who never go anywhere. When winter comes, they hibernate, waking up thinner in the spring.

CALIFORNIA
3,500 km
↓ (2,175 miles)

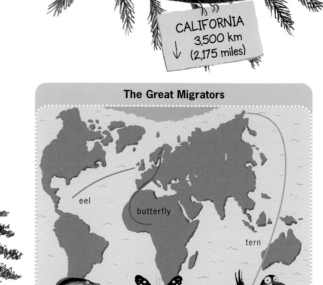

The Great Migrators

eel
butterfly
tern

Eel	Painted lady butterfly	Arctic tern
6,000 km	10,000 km	20,000 km
(3,730 miles)	(6,215 miles)	(12,430 miles)
one way	one way	one way

Pacific Ocean
300–400 km
(185–250 miles)
←

Some **lemmings** wander, while others bury themselves underground. Every forty years, there are 2,000 times as many of them. They migrate in all directions. Most of them die along the way.

The leatherback turtle doesn't migrate with the seasons. It just lets itself be carried by the same currents that carry the jellyfish it loves to eat. It will dive 1,000 m (3,280 ft.) to catch jellyfish.

HAWAIIAN COAST
← 4,500 km
(2,795 miles)

This scene shows the beginning of winter in **northwestern Canada**. Soon there will be hardly any animals left. Hundreds of species migrate, each with their own rythms according to the seasons.

Some **bats** hibernate. Their body temperature drops and their heart rate slows way down. That's how they preserve their stength as they live off their own body fat.

The sanderling sandpiper has spent the summer in Greenland. It joins the flock heading along the coastline.

VANCOUVER
← 300-400 km
(185-250 miles)

Grizzlies sleep the winter away in their dens. The females give birth to two to four cubs in January.

The caribou will soon be on the move. They will walk day and night. Only the females will stop to give birth. It will be dangerous, as the wolves are watching.

Number Crunch

10 billion: how many crickets migrate at the same time.

30,000 km (18,640 miles) is how far the grey-beaked puffin travels each year.

80 % is how much of its own weight an average bird loses after migrating.

50 % of animals that migrate die on the way.

Some **grey whales** spend the winter eating invertebrates off the sea floor. In spring, they travel to warm waters off the coast of Mexico to reproduce.

Salmon don't migrate with the seasons. They are born in a river, become adults at sea, and then travel back to the river, which they recognize by its scent, to reproduce.

GULF OF CALIFORNIA
3,000 km
(1,865 miles)

NORTH PACIFIC SIBERIAN COAST →
2,000 km (1,245 miles)

77

Animal Talk

Animals "talk" to each other in many different ways. That's why they use cries, colors, smells, mimicry, and gestures to communicate.

When **a bee** has scouted out a flower full of nectar, it returns to the hive and does a dance. There are different kinds of dances, depending on whether the flower is near or far away.

Hippopotamuses live in groups, spending their days immersed in water and their nights grazing on the riverbanks. If they sense danger, they moo.

Zebras live in herds, which sometime include gnus and antelopes. They have really good hearing, and if they pick up a distant threat, they whinny to disperse the herd.

Wolves howl at the Moon in chorus to let other packs know they are there, and to avoid fighting over the same prey.

If **a polecat** feels threatened or sick, it releases a disgusting odor through its anal glands like a skunk does. The polecat also uses this smelly message as a way to let other polecats know it's there.

Dingoes live in packs, like wolves. And like wolves, they use body postures to express their social standing. Lowering the head, for example, shows submission.

The weasel leaves a pile of feces outside his burrow to let everyone know it belongs to him.

When **an ant** finds food, it goes back to the anthill, leaving a fragrant chemical trail behind as it goes. That way, its fellow ants can follow the trail back to the food source.

Animals exchange information with members of their own species, as well as with other kinds of animals. They use sight, sound, touch, and smell as signals to identify themselves, warn of danger, point the way to food, mark a territory, and relieve tensions.

Starlings sing to call thousands of their kind together in trees or on electrical wires when it's time to migrate.

To intimidate a rival, **a male gorilla** roars and tears up shrubs, then rises up on his hind legs and pounds his chest.

The fox is an omnivore, who needs a lot of space to hunt for food. It marks its territory with smelly urine.

Octopuses change color to camouflage themselves, intimidate a rival, express their emotions, and show their love for a potential mate.

In a group of **marmots**, one will be a scout, exploring the surroundings and whistling if there is danger.

Like all cats, **lynx** lick each other a lot. It lowers their aggressions and relieves tension.

Rhesus monkeys mimic each other's facial expressions. A pout attracts attention.

Dik-dik antelopes mark their territory by rubbing the glands they have under their eyes against grass stalks.

79

Life in Groups

Many animals live in groups, and some belong to highly organized societies.

The termite hill is under attack. The drones hide in the middle and the soldiers move to the **front.** Though they have enormous jaws to defend themselves, many will die. If the attack is foiled, the drones will repair the damage.

There's an area where the drones **grow mushrooms.** Termites eat the mushrooms to help digest the wood and cellulose plants that make up their main diet.

As soon as eggs are laid, the drones take them to the termite **nursery.** When the larvae hatch, the drones feed them with a paste of regurgitated wood and plants.

The **royal chamber** is the first part of the termite hill that the drones build. This is where the king and queen live and reproduce. The queen can lay as many as 30,000 eggs a day.

A group of about 80 **chimpanzees** lives in a clearing in a tropical African forest next to a termite hill. The termites are their main food, along with leaves and stalks.

Chimpanzees pass on knowledge to one another. Here, a chimpanzee mother **teaches** her young one to push a stick into the termite hill to catch termites for a tasty meal.

Social insects, like ants, bees, and termites live in organizations where the role of each individual is strictly defined. Other animals, like monkeys and wolves, live in looser groups. Why live in groups? There's strength in numbers against predators, in claiming territory, hunting for food, and sharing tasks. The downside is that the group needs to eat a lot, which means moving often in search of new food sources.

A **dominant male** leads the group. His power is real, but flexible. Other males constantly challenge him.

Within the group, adults often **groom each other** for fleas. It's a way of lowering aggression and limiting conflict.

Chimpanzees **communicate** with mimicry and posturing. The male on the left is picking a fight.

The chimpanzee **can make tools.** This one has made a sponge out of moss and leaves. It collects water, which the chimpanzee drinks.

The termite hill is a complicated structure made up of rooms and passageways, as well as a cooling system. It's occupied by millions of individual termites, each one with a specific task. The highest termite hills are about 6 m (20 ft.) tall.

In southern Africa, **meerkats** live in colonies. Several families share burrows connected by passageways. Their social life is highly organized.

In tropical Africa, **weaver birds** live in huge colonies. So many bird couples have woven and tied their nests to this acacia tree that it's been turned into a natural high-rise apartment complex.

Courtship

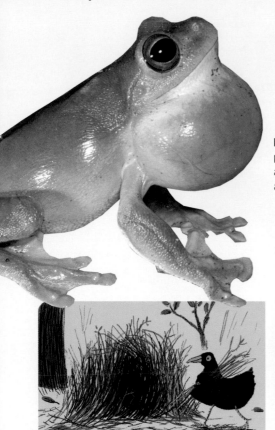

Male frogs and **toads** puff up their vocal cords and sing in a chorus to attract females.

Animals only reproduce at certain times of the year. Males pull out all the stops to attract females. It's called the mating dance.

The male **satin bowerbird** is a terrific architect. He builds a complicated nest made up of two rows of twigs.

He's a designer and decorator, too. He brightens up the nest with shiny blue objects to attract a female.

He does a dance holding something blue in his beak. A female approaches. He invites her inside by offering her the blue treasure.

A stag shrieks and bellows. Other stags answer him. It's a way of intimidating rivals and attracting females.

Two males want the same female. They fight each other by locking horns in a battle of power and dominance.

He does a dance...

The female goes with the winner. If he has won, it means that he is strong and has endurance, two good qualities for a future father!

A male **scorpion** shows off his claws to a female. He tries to impress her by spreading them apart so they will seem bigger.

The male and the female approach each other. The male blocks the female's path so she won't sting him, and he can take her where he wants to mate.

They lock onto each other with their claws. They dance back and forth for hours, even days, before mating.

A female animal often has a choice between several possible suitors, so the males have to compete to win her favor. Males seek to be recognized, and to be noticed. Each one wants to prove that he is in good health, and to make the female want him. How do they do that? Each male has his own a method: he may sing, show off brilliant colors, puff himself up, get into fights, or offer presents.

The **peacock** opens up his long tailfeathers with colorful eye-like markings. Then he struts in front of the female.

The male **firefly** gives off flashes of light from his stomach. How many there are and what color indicates what species he is.

When a female from the same species recognizes his code, she flashes out a signal that allows the male to identify her.

The male goes toward the female, guided by her flashing lights. If there is danger, she goes dark.

A male **arctic tern** has found a female. He circles her, crying out, then lands next to her and flaps his wings.

But the dance doesn't stop there. He flies out to sea and catches fish, which he brings back to her without ever landing.

He does this several times to convince her that he will be faithful and that he can provide food for their babies.

A male **elephant** ready to mate trumpets the news. A gland on his forehead releases an oily liquid. The smell attracts females.

If two such males should meet, they battle ferociously with their trunks, feet, and tusks to win the mate.

The elephant that loses takes off. The female accepts the courtship of the winner. They are going to mate.

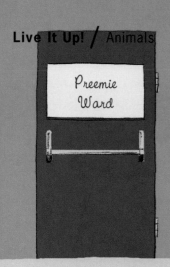

Preemie
Ward

Having Babies

In order for an animal species to survive, its members must have babies. Some animals have big bunches of little ones, others have only a few.

Maternity
Ward

While most snakes lay their eggs, the **boa constrictor** carries her eggs inside her body. She gives birth to between 10 and 50 babies.

A **great white shark** mother also carries its eggs inside herself, as do most sharks. She has between 1 and 9 babies. Other kinds of sharks, like the lemon shark, do lay their eggs.

After a pregnancy of 15 months, the **giraffe** gives birth standing up. The baby giraffe falls to the ground from a great height. It has to be able to stand up right away and follow its mother.

Egg
Ward

The echidna and the duck-billed platypus are the only mammals that lay eggs. The female **platypus** lays between 1 and 3 eggs that it protects in a stomach pocket before taking them to her burrow.

A female **midwife toad** expels a strand of eggs, which a male toad fertilizes. The male then wraps the eggs around his thighs. He carries them this way for 3 weeks before bringing them into water, where the eggs will hatch.

The female **royal cobra** makes a nest in which she lays between 20 and 50 eggs. She covers them with grass. She and her mate watch over them until they hatch.

After five weeks of pregnancy, the female **red kangaroo** gives birth to an infant that weighs only 1 g (0.03 oz.) and is about 3 cm (1 ¼ in.) long. It crawls up to its mother's marsupial pouch where it will nurse for 6 months.

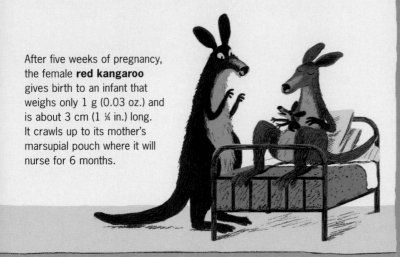

After a pregnancy of 22 months, a mother **elephant** has one baby that she will nurse for 3 years. An African baby elephant weighs 120 kg (265 lb.), while an Asian one weighs 100 kg (220 lb.).

The **cottontail rabbit** can give birth 4 or 5 times a year. Each litter has 3 to 8 bunnies. That's a lot of rabbits!

Having babies is different for different species.

Most mammals are viviparous. That means mammals' babies develop in their mothers' bellies and are born fully formed. The kangaroo, which is a marsupial, gives birth prematurely. Its baby will finish growing inside the mother's pouch. Birds are oviparous, which means they lay eggs that develop outside of their bodies. Some reptiles are ovoviviparous; their eggs develop inside the mother.

The female **seahorse** lays her eggs in the belly of the male. He will fertilize the eggs and keep them warm until they hatch. Baby seahorses are born fully formed.

The female **Nile crocodile** lays between 25 to 100 eggs in holes dug into the sandy banks of a river. When they're ready to hatch, the babies cry out and their mother helps break their shells.

The albatross mates for life. The female lays a single egg each year, or once every two years. Mother and father take turns sitting on it for 80 days.

The female **octopus** hatches 100,000 eggs that hang from the roof of her shelter. She watches over them and cleans them for 3 months. When the eggs hatch, she dies.

Pampered Kids

When a **golden eaglet** is born, the parents work together to feed the baby and, at 10 weeks old, push it out of the nest. Then they teach the eaglet how to hunt and feed itself.

Some animal parents take their time feeding, caring for, and protecting their little ones before allowing them to fend for themselves.

A mother **koala** has only one baby, which she nurses in her pouch for 6 months. After that, the little one rides on her back and eats eucalyptus leaves pre-chewed by its mother. At 11 months, the baby can live on its own.

In her den, the **panther** gives birth to one to six cubs, which are born blind. She nurses them for 3 months. Then she shows them how to hunt and live on their own. Those who survive leave their mother at 22 months.

In a **wolf pack**, only the dominant couple has babies. The mother has four to seven blind cubs that she nurses in her den. The cubs learn to hunt with the other members of the pack. They become real hunters when they are about 6 months old.

A female **baboon** has one baby that she nurses until another one is born. All the female baboons in a troop help take care of the babies. The young females stay with their mothers, while the males leave when they reach adolescence.

Certain baby animals need their parents in order to survive. Depending on the species, they are cared for by their mother, both parents, or the whole group they belong to. Some parents are happy to feed their kids for as long as it takes, while others spend their time teaching. They show the young ones how to hunt, how to get along with other members of the group, and how to watch out for predators so they can learn how to survive on their own.

Why do some parents not look after their little ones ?

It doesn't mean that they are bad parents, just that they don't have what it takes to be a parent. For example, to feed a baby, an animal would have to hunt a lot for enough food. And to protect a baby for a long time, an animal would have to be able to stand up to predators. Both of these require a lot of energy that some animals just don't have. But to make up for this, their babies tend to be born fully formed, and are able to take care of themselves from the moment they arrive.

A mother **crocodile** raises her babies until they can hunt on their own. She carries them in her mouth and throat to keep them safe from predators.

Alone from the start!

A **sea turtle** abandons her eggs on the beach. As soon as they're born, the babies have to dash into the sea to escape predators.

Most frogs leave their eggs in the water. If the eggs aren't eaten by fish, they will hatch into **tadpoles** that will become frogs.

A **butterfly caterpillar** hatches from an egg that its mother abandoned on a leaf. It will feed itself before turning into a butterfly.

It's the male **emperor penguin** that sits on the egg. When the fledgling hatches, the female feeds it and protects it from the cold by holding it against her belly. At the age of 40 days, the baby bird joins a penguin daycare that is protected from predators and the cold by a circle of the adults.

A **shrew** can have 10 little ones. She nurses them for several weeks. When they go for a walk, they sometimes form a train, each one using its teeth to hold the tail of the one in front. It's a good way to not get lost!

A baby **pink flamingo** stays in the nest for several days, before going to flamingo daycare. The parents feed it food they have regurgitated until it grows flight feathers and can hunt on its own.

KNOW-IT-ALL NEWS

Vera Smart
Editor-in-chief

* * *

Ashley Asks
Interviewer

* * *

Tex A. Snap
Photo Journalist

* * *

Claire Itty
Researcher

* * *

Art Phul
Illustrator

* * *

Ed Shorter
News Briefs

From the Editor's Desk

Like the gorilla, orangutan, and chimpanzee, the bonobo is one of the great apes. Mother and child stay together and remain emotionally attached. Their relationship helps to make these apes very sensitive and may explain why they have such a peaceful existence.

Vera Smart

Ashley Asks

Scientist Sue Hennington studies how language and sounds are learned. She works with apes, including the famous bonobo Xanxi.

Can you tell us about Xanxi and his amazing abilities?
Xanxi is a male bonobo who is about 15 years old and has always lived in captivity. Since he was very young, he's been learning to recognize symbols on a keyboard for things (such as a strawberry) or actions (such as "to give"). Today, he knows about 200 symbols. He knows how to carry out orders of several symbols together, like "give —

Well-Behaved Bonobos

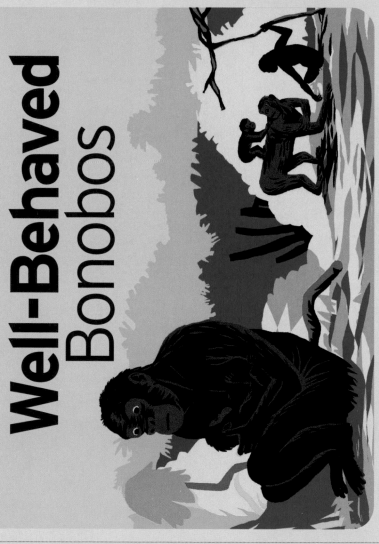

This baby bonobo has just been born. He's going to get a lot of attention and affection from his mother. She's going to nurse him, of course, but she's also going to pick out his fleas, look into his eyes, and hug him. It's a good way to grow up without stress. His growth will be very slow. His mother will carry him close to her chest at first, and later on her back.

Vera Smart

Art Phul

strawberry — dog." Xanxi also understands English very well.

Can he talk?

He makes certain sounds. But it's a long way from language. It's more like vocalizations. Xanxi knows if an order is addressed to him or one of his relatives. And if the relative doesn't respond, Xanxi is capable of trying to make her understand. He also watches television. But you need to realize that Xanxi is exceptional.

Birth Notice

Mama Bonobo is pleased to introduce: *BANABO !* It's a boy! We will stay together our whole lives.

Tex A. Snap

Mother and Child

The mother

• She has her first baby when she is 13 to 15 years old.

• She has one baby every 4 or 5 years, after she stops nursing the previous one.

1st baby 15 years old   **2nd baby** 20 years old

• Pregnancy lasts about 8 months.

The baby

• At birth, weighs 1.36 kg (3 lbs.)

1.36 kg

• Adult weight:

Female 37 kg (82 lbs.)   **Male** 41 kg (90 lbs.)

• Reaches adult size at about 14 to 16 years old.

• Life expectancy:

 50 to 55 years old

Claire Itty

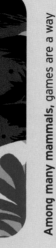

When the baby is 4 years old, his mother stops nursing him. But she will still take care of him. Here, a mother is going to share fruit with her baby, who is begging her for it by holding out his hands. The one in the back has just been weaned, so she's sucking her thumb.

Among many mammals, games are a way of teaching and learning. The little ones play with each other or with the adults. The bonobos play with a real sense of humor. They seem to smile, laugh, and make fun of themselves.

In the African forest, danger is everywhere. These young ones have wandered off and gotten themselves stuck in a muddy puddle. Fortunately, a female adult has found them. She yells and waves her arms to get the other adult females to come and help. A leopard watches it all.

Tex A. Snap

Eating Matters

Animals can't live without food. But they don't all like the same things or have the same diet. What they eat determines how they look.

The **sloth bear** and the **mandrill** are omnivores. This a huge advantage: they can almost always find something to eat.

There are more herbivores than other kinds of animals. **Herbivores** eat leaves, grass, seeds, and fruit. Some of them are very particular, like the panda that eats only bamboo shoots. Herbivores are often hunted by **carnivores**, which eat meat, fish, and insects. There are other animals that eat everything—these are the **omnivores**. Carrion feeders, like the hyena, and scavengers, like the earthworm, make do with animals and plants that are dead. When they eat, they clean up the world.

● A **vulture** tears at flesh with its big beak. Its long neck and featherless head allow the vulture to stick its head into a cadaver's belly without getting blood all over itself.

● A **lobster** uses its large claw to break mollusk shells, crustacean carapaces, and fish bones. Its little claw is for cutting flesh.

● A **chicken** pecks at grains with her beak. She has no teeth, so she doesn't chew. But she swallows gravel that grinds up the grain in her crop, a pocket on her neck.

● The **squirrel** is a rodent that eats seeds, nuts, and fruit. When winter is coming, the squirrel stocks up on its food supply.

● The **manatee**, also called a sea cow, grazes on aquatic plants in the sea or in the estuaries of rivers. As soon as her molars wear down, she grows more.

● The **vampire bat** of South America drinks the blood of mammals and birds by piercing their skin with its sharp teeth. Its saliva keeps the small wound from healing.

● A **reticulated python** strangles a young antelope by tightly encircling it. With its supple jaws, the python can swallow it whole. Then it spends weeks digesting the meal.

● An **earthworm** digs tunnels in the earth and swallows soil. It eats rotten vegetable matter and turns it into humus, creating fertile soil.

● The **hyena** feeds on animals that larger predators have killed and left behind. Its powerful jaws crush bones to get at the marrow.

Garbage Eaters' Menu
● Carrion
● Earth

Herbivore Menu
● Fruits
● Grasses
● Seeds

Carnivore Menu
● Insects
● Fish
● Meat
● Blood

● The **giant Australian fruit bat** loves all kinds of fruit. Its sharp canine teeth, wide molars, and powerful jaw allow it to chew through the toughest skins.

● The **pelican** uses its beak like a fish net. It stocks the fish it has caught in the bottom part of its beak.

● Some **leeches** can live for half a year without eating. This worm attaches itself to an animal and sucks its blood—often enough to store in its body for 6 months.

● The **African wild dog** is a very capable carnivore. It can kill prey bigger than itself, like a gnu. It hunts in packs that stick to well-defined roles.

● A **sea otter** pries open the shells of sea urchins and other mollusks by using its front paws to smash the shell against a rock placed on its stomach.

A **cow** grazes on the grass of a meadow or on dried grass (hay). She ruminates. That means she partly digests her food in her stomach, then brings it up before swallowing again.

● An **anteater** digs a hole into an ant hill or termite hill with its claws, and then sticks its very long tongue down inside. The tongue is coated with gluey saliva that catches the insects.

Eat or Be Eaten

In the wild, animals use different methods to hunt and eat. They also use a lot of tricks to avoid being eaten!

The green **iguana** is well hidden in the leaves. It hides in order to hunt and has spotted a beetle on the branch.

❖ The orange **sawyer beetle** is easy to see. But in nature, this bright color can signal "I'm poisonous!"

The jaguar's spotted coat camouflages it well in the shifting light of the underbrush. This super-predator watches for prey on the ground or in the trees. The jaguar is also an excellent swimmer.

With wings folded, **the leaf grasshopper** looks just like a leaf. Once it has been spotted, it tries to frighten the predator by opening its wings and revealing round circles that look like very disturbing eyes.

In its habitat, an animal preys on certain species. It also runs the risk of being eaten by other animals who consider it prey. All animals make up a food chain where each one is either predator (the eater) or prey (the eaten). At the top of the food chain are "superpredators" that fear nothing and will not be eaten. Unless a person comes by with a rifle, that is.

A carapace of thick scales protects the **giant armadillo.** When threatened it can burrow in an instant and hide itself, roll into a ball, or run away.

The trapdoor spider can sense the grasshopper's vibrations. The spider will leap on the grasshopper and grab it before injecting it with a strong poison.

The **Amazon Forest** in South America is home to the largest number of different species in the world. Here you'll find the most amazing variations of hunting methods and camouflage.

◄ **The red howler monkey's** yells are loud enough to be heard from far away. This lets the monkey warn its relatives when there's a jaguar around.

You'd think that the **macaw's** bright colors would make it easy to spot. But in fact, living in the tree tops where the light is bright and shines on its feathers, it's actually hard to see.

A sloth moves very slowly, so it's not very good at running away from a predator. What it does to protect itself is to let green algae grow on its coat as camouflage.

The coral snake has bands of bright color that make it recognizable. It is very poisonous, so most other animals leave it alone. Other non-poisonous snakes imitate this coloring so that they, too, won't be disturbed.

Poison-dart frogs can be bright blue, acid green, or red—a loud and strong message that they are deadly.

The capybara is the world's largest rodent. It eats aquatic plants along riverbanks and is a good swimmer. To escape a jaguar, it hides in the water, letting only its eyes, ears, and nostrils stick out.

A caiman looks like a dead tree trunk. You can only see its eyes and nostrils as it waits to ambush the capybara. It will pounce suddenly, dragging its prey underwater to drown.

Piranhas hunt in schools. They are carnivores who attack when they smell the blood of an animal that has been hurt. Their razor sharp teeth can strip a carcass bare.

Cool Critters!

The way animals look and behave is amazing. Here are a few examples of some pretty far out ones.

When the Sun's too strong, the **ground squirrel** lifts its tail up over itself like an umbrella.

A flying dragon lizard launches itself off a tree and glides through the air. Its "parachute" is a membrane that stretches between its legs.

Female **dung beetles** roll up some cow dung to feed their larvae back in the den.

Oxpeckers land on an **antelope** to eat parasites on its hide. Their cooperation guarantees that the antelope stays healthy and that the oxpeckers have something to eat.

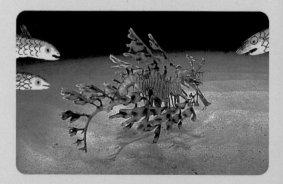

A **sea dragon** is an Australian sea horse with a skin that looks like algae. It's a great camouflage to keep the sea horse hidden and safe.

This **frog** is playing dead. Lying on its back, it slows down its heartbeat and stiffens. A good way to make a predator go away.

A young **kangaroo** is too big to fit into its mother's pouch. But it can still hide its head to feel safe and secure.

Leaf-cutter ants of South America are farmers. The leaves they carry to the anthill serve as growing beds for the mushrooms they raise.

A female **proboscis** monkey has a small turned-up nose. But the male has a real honker. It gets even bigger as he ages.

A **clownfish** is immune to the **sea anemone's** poisonous sting. So it nestles in the anemone to hide from predators. In return, it attracts small sea creatures that the anemone likes to eat.

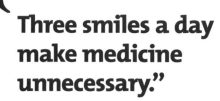

Understanding your body is an amazing trip! In a 1966 movie, appropriately titled *Fantastic Voyage*, five people shrunk to microscopic size travel by miniature submarine through the veins of a human being. Their mission: reach the brain to destroy a blood clot. Along their unbelievable trek they face terrible dangers, like an army of white blood cells and antibodies, that make their lives very difficult. A human body is a brilliantly functioning machine that doesn't like intruders and surprises....

Hang on, the next few pages are going to be a thrilling ride, too!

A human body keeps changing for its entire life span. This simple natural law is summed up beautifully in Greek mythology by a riddle the Sphinx asked Oedipus as the king was on his way to Thebes: "What animal walks on four legs in the morning, two at noon, and three in the evening?" The answer Oedipus gave was, "Man. He walks on four legs when he is a crawling infant, two legs as an adult, and leans on a cane in old age." The Greek myth tells us that Oedipus was the first person to answer the riddle correctly. In exchange, the Sphinx loosened her grip of terror on the city of Thebes.

The Human Body

In 1818, Mary Shelley wrote a novel about a scientist who made a living creature using parts from cadavers. But the doctor realized his creation was terrifying and ugly, so he turned his back on it. The monster, hurt by the rejection, vowed to take his revenge by killing all that was dear to his creator. He demanded a bride to share his life. The doctor saw he had no choice but to kill his creation, and himself, to make the nightmare end. The doctor's name was Victor Frankenstein.

Nature has given us two ears and only one tongue so that we can listen twice as much as we talk."

Greek proverb

Your body, as you know, has lots of things that come in pairs: two eyes, two ears, two lungs, two arms, two legs, and even two nostrils. According to a Catalan legend, the first people had all that, times two again! They were made up of two bodies twisted together in the form of a cross. One person was both male and female and could make babies alone. But they made too many babies too quickly, so it was decided to split them into two. And that's why, when we're looking for love, we say we are looking for our "other half."

Without a body you simply wouldn't exist! You need your body to hold your skeleton and organs in place. But your body also allows you to interact with the outside world. It lets you taste, touch, smell, see, hear, feel hot and cold, communicate with others, and explore everything that's around you.

How We're Made

A **skeleton's** bones form an articulated framework. The articulation, or joints, between bones is what allows the skeleton to move.

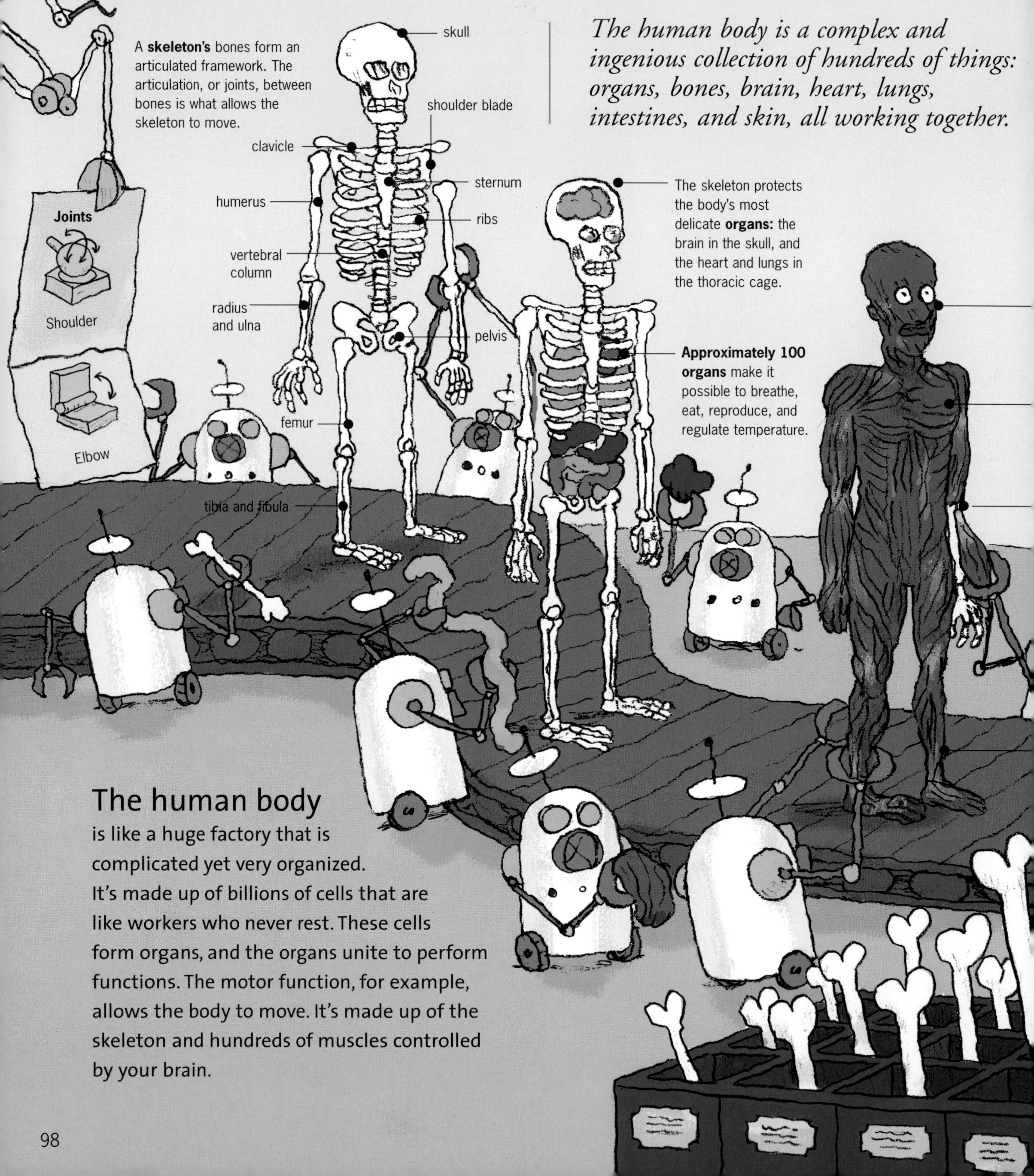

The human body is a complex and ingenious collection of hundreds of things: organs, bones, brain, heart, lungs, intestines, and skin, all working together.

- skull
- shoulder blade
- clavicle
- sternum
- humerus
- ribs
- vertebral column
- radius and ulna
- pelvis
- femur
- tibia and fibula

Joints

Shoulder

Elbow

The skeleton protects the body's most delicate **organs:** the brain in the skull, and the heart and lungs in the thoracic cage.

Approximately 100 organs make it possible to breathe, eat, reproduce, and regulate temperature.

The human body

is like a huge factory that is complicated yet very organized. It's made up of billions of cells that are like workers who never rest. These cells form organs, and the organs unite to perform functions. The motor function, for example, allows the body to move. It's made up of the skeleton and hundreds of muscles controlled by your brain.

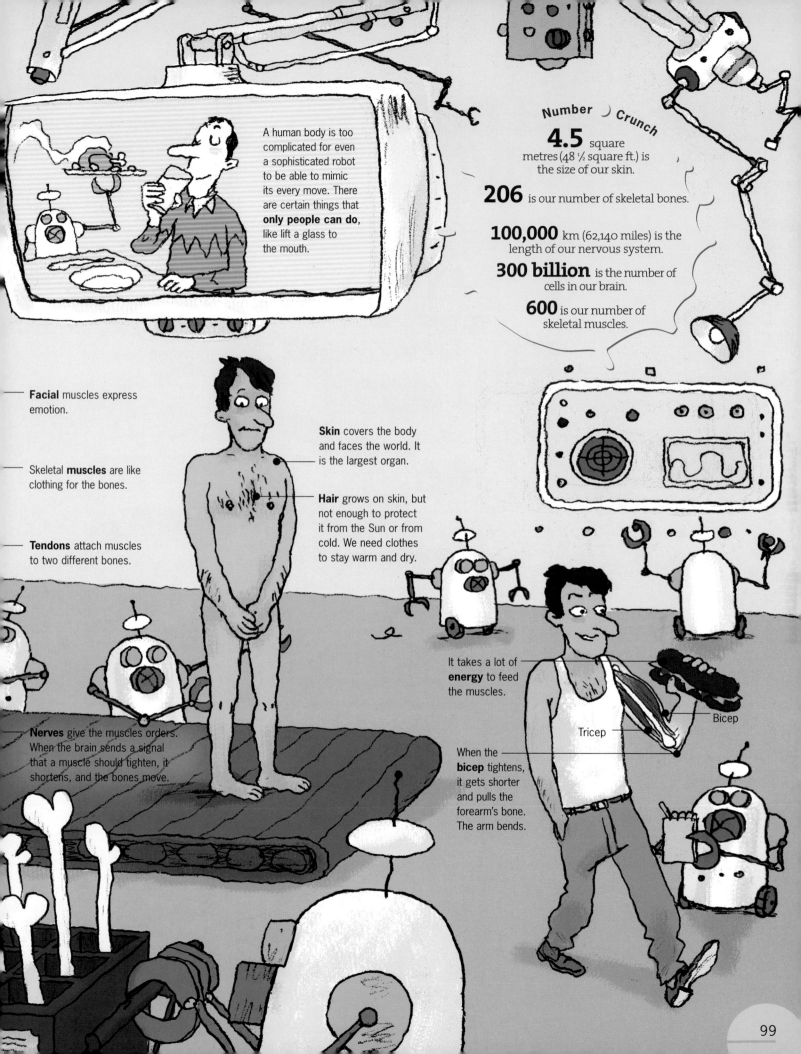

A human body is too complicated for even a sophisticated robot to be able to mimic its every move. There are certain things that **only people can do**, like lift a glass to the mouth.

Number Crunch

4.5 square metres (48 ½ square ft.) is the size of our skin.

206 is our number of skeletal bones.

100,000 km (62,140 miles) is the length of our nervous system.

300 billion is the number of cells in our brain.

600 is our number of skeletal muscles.

Facial muscles express emotion.

Skeletal **muscles** are like clothing for the bones.

Tendons attach muscles to two different bones.

Skin covers the body and faces the world. It is the largest organ.

Hair grows on skin, but not enough to protect it from the Sun or from cold. We need clothes to stay warm and dry.

Nerves give the muscles orders. When the brain sends a signal that a muscle should tighten, it shortens, and the bones move.

It takes a lot of **energy** to feed the muscles.

Bicep

Tricep

When the **bicep** tightens, it gets shorter and pulls the forearm's bone. The arm bends.

99

Eat—and Build That Body!

Before food can be used by the body as a building block or fuel, it needs to be transformed through a process called digestion.

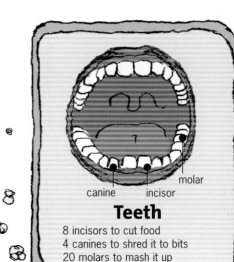

Teeth

8 incisors to cut food
4 canines to shred it to bits
20 molars to mash it up

canine   incisor   molar

Mouth

Our **teeth** take food and cut it, shred it, mash it, and coat it with saliva. That makes it easier for food to go down the **esophagus**, the first part of the digestive plumbing.

Esophagus

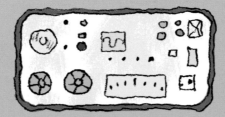

What we eat builds our body and makes it work. Foods belong in different groups according to their nutritional contributions. Meat and other protein sources, such as eggs, fish, and dairy products are necessary for our body to grow and to heal itself. Cereals, such as rice and wheat, starches (like potatoes and lentils), and fats provide energy to our systems. What we drink helps the body replace the water it uses and loses every day.

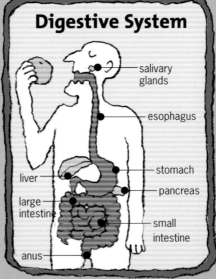

Digestive System

salivary glands
esophagus
liver
stomach
pancreas
large intestine
small intestine
anus

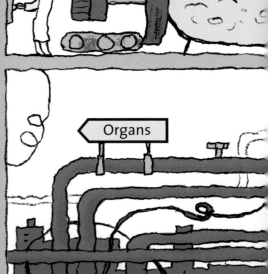

Organs

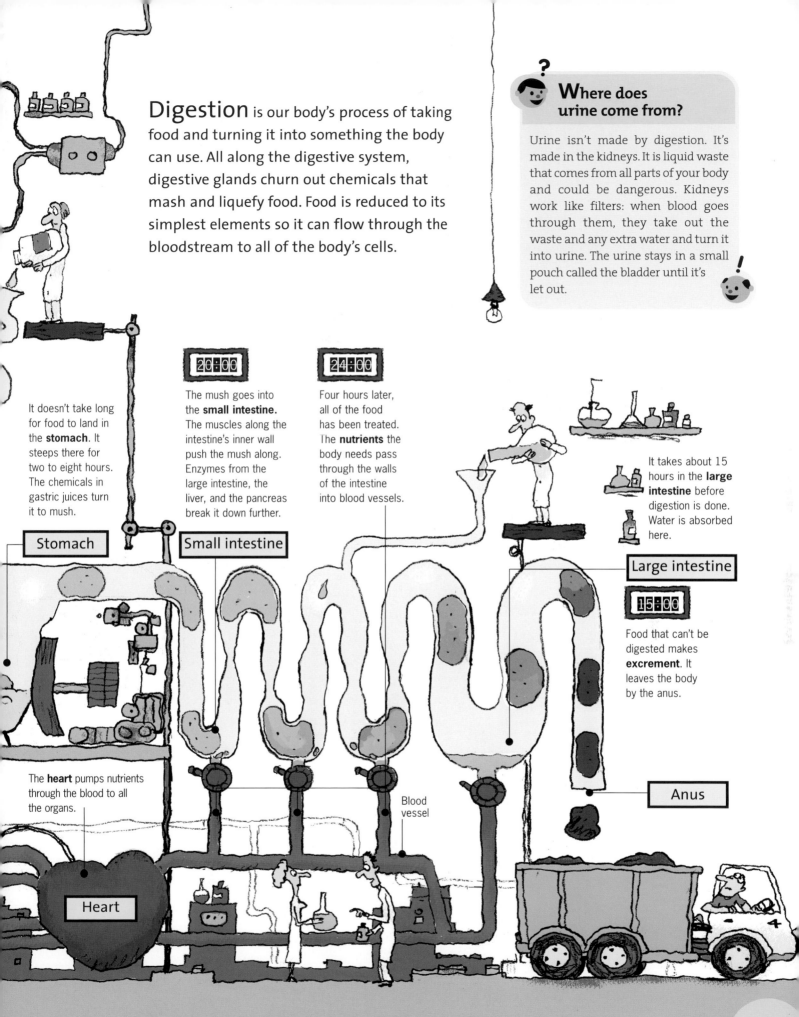

Digestion is our body's process of taking food and turning it into something the body can use. All along the digestive system, digestive glands churn out chemicals that mash and liquefy food. Food is reduced to its simplest elements so it can flow through the bloodstream to all of the body's cells.

Where does urine come from?

Urine isn't made by digestion. It's made in the kidneys. It is liquid waste that comes from all parts of your body and could be dangerous. Kidneys work like filters: when blood goes through them, they take out the waste and any extra water and turn it into urine. The urine stays in a small pouch called the bladder until it's let out.

20:00

The mush goes into the **small intestine.** The muscles along the intestine's inner wall push the mush along. Enzymes from the large intestine, the liver, and the pancreas break it down further.

24:00

Four hours later, all of the food has been treated. The **nutrients** the body needs pass through the walls of the intestine into blood vessels.

It doesn't take long for food to land in the **stomach.** It steeps there for two to eight hours. The chemicals in gastric juices turn it to mush.

It takes about 15 hours in the **large intestine** before digestion is done. Water is absorbed here.

Stomach

Small intestine

Large intestine

15:00

Food that can't be digested makes **excrement.** It leaves the body by the anus.

The **heart** pumps nutrients through the blood to all the organs.

Blood vessel

Anus

Heart

Breath Is Life

Using the 950 km (590 miles) of blood vessels in the body, billions of red blood cells carry oxygen throughout the entire organism. The heart keeps them moving.

Breathe in, breathe out! Whether we're awake or asleep, without thinking about it, we are using our respiratory system. That's the way we constantly move air in and out of our lungs. This is where the oxygen that is in the air—and that is vital to human life—is extracted. Then the blood takes over. The heart beats regularly to keep the blood moving, bringing oxygen to all the body's cells. When we breathe out, we rid the body of carbon dioxide and complete the cycle of respiration.

career

air monitor
This new career is important for the quality of life, especially in a city where factories and cars emit harmful pollutants. Specialists are needed to measure air quality. If there is too much pollution, they alert the media and recommend that young children don't go outside and that people with breathing difficulties take it easy.

oxygen

LUNG

Each cell receives the **oxygen** it needs.

MUSCLE

The cells get rid of **carbon dioxide** and other waste.

In each organ, blood vessels branch out into smaller vessels, no wider than a hair. These are the **capillary vessels.**

Blood circulates slowly through the **capillary vessels**, giving each organ a chance to get its oxygen and get rid of its carbon dioxide waste.

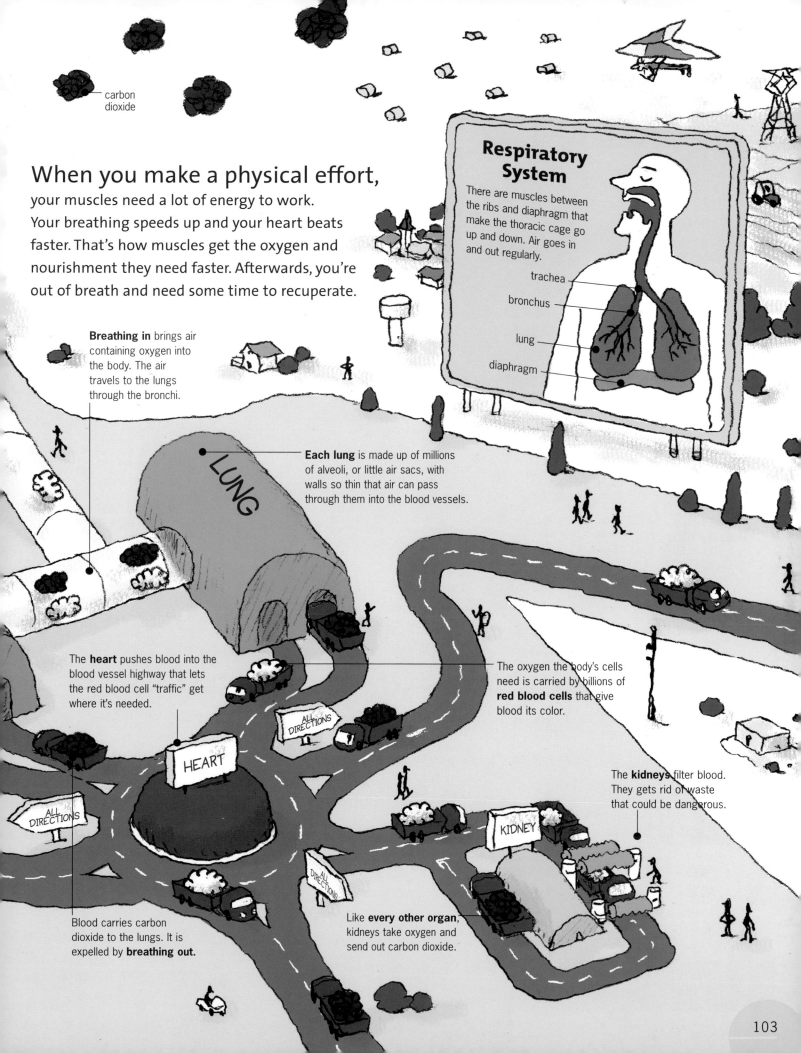

carbon dioxide

When you make a physical effort,

your muscles need a lot of energy to work. Your breathing speeds up and your heart beats faster. That's how muscles get the oxygen and nourishment they need faster. Afterwards, you're out of breath and need some time to recuperate.

Respiratory System

There are muscles between the ribs and diaphragm that make the thoracic cage go up and down. Air goes in and out regularly.

trachea

bronchus

lung

diaphragm

Breathing in brings air containing oxygen into the body. The air travels to the lungs through the bronchi.

LUNG

Each lung is made up of millions of alveoli, or little air sacs, with walls so thin that air can pass through them into the blood vessels.

The **heart** pushes blood into the blood vessel highway that lets the red blood cell "traffic" get where it's needed.

The oxygen the body's cells need is carried by billions of **red blood cells** that give blood its color.

ALL DIRECTIONS

HEART

ALL DIRECTIONS

The **kidneys** filter blood. They gets rid of waste that could be dangerous.

ALL DIRECTIONS

KIDNEY

Blood carries carbon dioxide to the lungs. It is expelled by **breathing out**.

Like **every other organ**, kidneys take oxygen and send out carbon dioxide.

The Five Senses

The senses play a vital role in our perception of the world. The sensory organs absorb stimuli and turn them into signals. Those signals travel along the sensory nerves to specific parts of the brain.

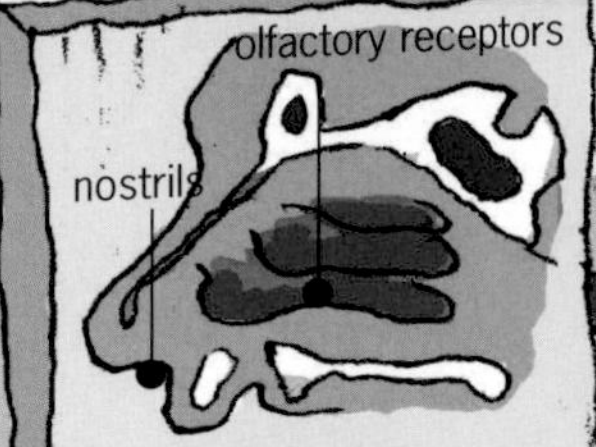

olfactory receptors

nostrils

Smell

Air full of scents reaches the inside of the **nose** and enters cavities covered with cells that are sensitive to odor.

A **dog** can smell 1,000 to 1 million times better than a person.

Taste and **smell** are tied to each other. A stuffed nose makes it hard to properly taste what you're eating.

Sensations go to the **brain**. Information is received and compared to stored memory, then interpreted.

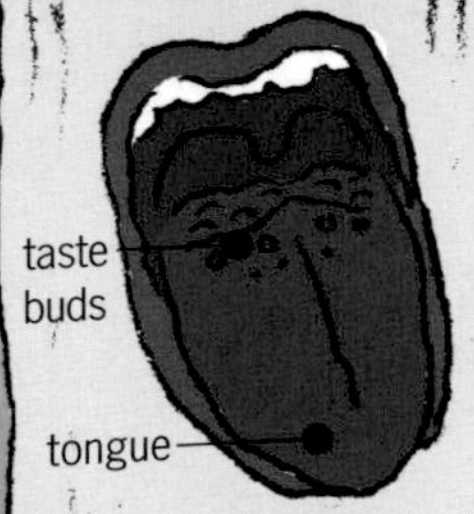

taste buds

tongue

Taste

Taste buds on the **tongue** can recognize four flavors: sweet, salty, sour, and bitter.

Sight, hearing, touch, smell, and taste: our five
senses are our connection to the world outside. Receptors in the eye and ear can pick up messages from far away. The olfactory cells in the nose and taste buds in the mouth react to chemical substances. The skin's sensory organs react to direct contact with the body.

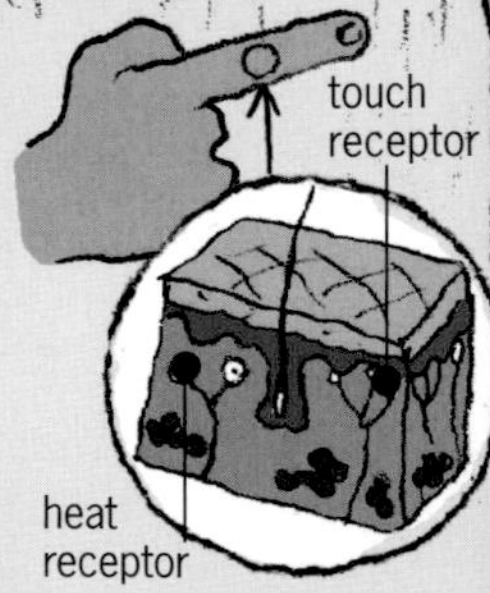

touch receptor

heat receptor

Touch

Sensors spread all over the **skin** make it possible to feel touch.

104

What happens when a sense doesn't work?

Living with sensory deprivation makes it difficult to discover the world and communicate. There are ways to handle this, depending on which sense is missing. There are tools that can be used or methods that can be learned. For example, the Braille alphabet, a series of raised dots, lets a blind person read, while sign language helps deaf and mute people communicate.

Brain

cornea
pupil
retina
lens
optic nerve

Sight
Millions of receptors on the retina in the **eye** capture light and color. These signals are sent to the brain by the optic nerve.

Because we have two eyes, we can see in **dimensions** and can **estimate distance.**

Eye glasses or contact lenses can correct certain vision problems.

Someone who is **blind** may strengthen his other senses.

The **inner ear** is very delicate and can be damaged by loud noise.

hammer and anvil
auditory nerve
ear drum
cochlea
← inner ear →

Hearing
Sounds go into the ear and make the ear drum **vibrate**. These vibrations are transmitted into the inner ear by the hammer and anvil, where they are turned into signals sent by the auditory nerve.

Some parts of the body, like the palm of the hand and the **fingertips**, are very sensitive. It's normal. They're full of sensors.

The **skin** is sensitive to temperature, pressure, and pain.

We can recognize a face by **touch,** and feel when someone touches us.

Nine Months to Birth

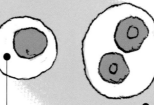

1+1=1. That's how a couple who love each other can make a baby. And how two reproductive cells can join with each other to create a fertilized egg whose cells divide and multiply to become an embryo.

The mother makes an **egg.** The father contributes millions of **sperm.**

A single sperm penetrates the egg to **fertilize it.**

The fertilized egg splits into 2, 4, 8, then 16 cells to become an **embryo**, which implants itself in the **uterus.** The uterus is a smooth, stretchy muscle inside a woman's belly.

outer uterine wall

placenta

amniotic fluid

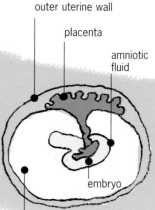

embryo

At three weeks, the embryo is protected by a sac of **amniotic fluid.** It is the size of a grain of wheat, with a heart that has begun to beat. The **umbilical cord** keeps it attached to the mother. Nutrients necessary for development enter the placenta through the umbilical cord.

We're having a baby! For many couples, these are some of the happiest words they will ever say to each other. It's the beginning of an amazing change as a new life has begun to grow inside a pregnant woman.

By the Numbers

133 million How many babies are born each year.

247 How many babies are born each minute.

4 How many babies are born each second.

7.16 The number of babies born per woman in Niger, which has the highest fertility rate in the world.

2.06 The number of babies born per woman in the United States, which ranks as 118th on the list.

1.64 The number of babies born per woman in Canada, which ranks 159th.

1.16 The number of babies born per woman in Singapore, which ranks lowest of 192 countries.

It all begins at fertilization,

when the father's sperm meets the mother's egg. The sperm enters the egg and the two together become a fertilized egg. Each reproductive cell in the egg carries half of the information needed to grow a full baby. It already knows if it will be a boy or a girl. The egg divides rapidly and then the embryo becomes attached securely in the mother's belly. There it grows bit by bit, taking nine months to become fully formed.

How are twins born?

Sometimes, a mother produces two eggs that are fertilized at the same time. These will become two embryos that will be born as fraternal twins. They will be the same age, possibly the same sex, but they will look different. Sometimes a single fertilized egg splits into two embryos and becomes two babies who are the same sex and look exactly alike. They are called identical twins.

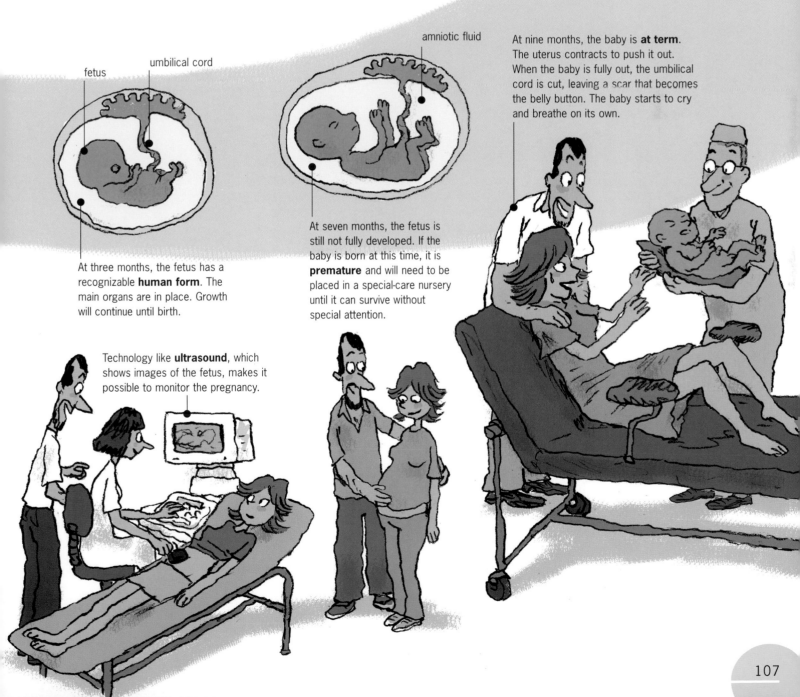

amniotic fluid

fetus

umbilical cord

At three months, the fetus has a recognizable **human form**. The main organs are in place. Growth will continue until birth.

At seven months, the fetus is still not fully developed. If the baby is born at this time, it is **premature** and will need to be placed in a special-care nursery until it can survive without special attention.

At nine months, the baby is **at term**. The uterus contracts to push it out. When the baby is fully out, the umbilical cord is cut, leaving a scar that becomes the belly button. The baby starts to cry and breathe on its own.

Technology like **ultrasound**, which shows images of the fetus, makes it possible to monitor the pregnancy.

Slices of Life

Childhood, adolescence, adulthood, old age: each part of life has its own changes, experiences, and challenges.

Until the age of **3 months**, a baby sleeps a lot. She nurses with her mother or takes milk from a bottle.

Measles, mumps, chicken pox: these **childhood diseases** aren't usually serious but can be contagious.

At **3 years old**, a child might be in nursery school. He can talk well.

SCHOOL

All through childhood, the body grows and changes slowly. A child develops an ability to learn and a desire to explore. At around age 11 or 12, growth speeds up and several changes take place, such as hair appearing on different parts of the body. These are the first signs of puberty. The little girl or little boy is bit by bit becoming a young woman or young man.

Keeping mentally and physically active helps makes **old age** more comfortable.

Starting at about **8 months**, an infant makes sounds, can sit up, crawls on all fours, and touches everything!

Between **10 and 18 months**, a toddler learns to walk alone, eat with a spoon, and understands several words.

At **4 years old**, a child is more coordinated and can ride a tricycle.

At **6**, a child learns to read and write. He has his first permanent tooth.

108

TOOTHIFUL with flouride

To be in good health means feeling well both in your body and in your mind. Good hygiene, a balanced diet, exercise, and feeling loved all contribute to being well.

KewlKlothes

DR. OUCH

Vaccines protect us from illnesses that could be serious.

Becoming an **adolescent** brings lots of changes to your body.

Young people discover feelings of love and pair off into **couples**.

At puberty, girls develop breasts. Boys' voices become lower.

To be permanently or temporarily **disabled** means making adjustments in day-to-day life.

A body can hurt, as the result of an accident or sickness. The loss of the use of a limb, or limited mobility, can make day-to-day life more difficult. The right care and the support of other people can help you get healthy again. But as the years go by, the body ages and gets tired more easily. Older people may slow down but they still have a lot to share!

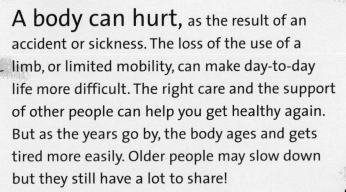

Sport is good for health, and also builds self-esteem and respect for others.

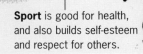

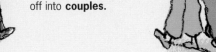

KNOW-IT-ALL NEWS

Vera Smart
Editor-in-chief

Ashley Asks
Interviewer

Tex A. Snap
Photo Journalist

Claire Itty
Researcher

Art Phul
Illustrator

Ed Shorter
News Briefs

From the Editor's Desk

Malaria is the number one parasite-caused illness in the world today. The parasite that causes it is carried by the female anopheles mosquito. One third of the world's population lives in high-risk areas, most often found in developing countries. Vera Smart

Hunting Malaria: The Illness Returns!

It has been known for a long time that living in warm and humid places creates the risk of malaria, or "swamp fever." It was also proved that drying out a swamp reduced the number of people who got sick, but no one knew why. Where did the illness come from? The air? Something else?

In 1880, a French army doctor in Algeria named Alphonse Laveran proved that the illness isn't caused by water or the air in swamps. He observed that the blood of a sick person was infected by a parasite, the plasmodium, that killed off red blood cells. But how was the parasite transmitted?

Art Phul

Ashley Asks

Kofi is 9 years old. He's a student in Ghana, in Western Africa.

Hello, Kofi. You have malaria and you regularly experience bouts of it. Can you tell us what it's like?
The bouts are very hard on me. They start very quickly. For no apparent reason, I suddenly feel sick and weak. Every little thing bothers me—even the light, and the sound of my little sister's voice.

Is there a high fever?
Yes. All of a sudden I feel like I'm inside an iceberg. I shake

and shiver all over. Even being wrapped up with lots of blankets doesn't help. I sweat like crazy, but I feel like I'm made of ice.

Isn't there any medicine?
Yes. I'm lucky enough to live near a hospital, so a nurse can give me shots. It helps a bit.

Does the fever last a long time?
The fever spikes for several hours and keeps coming back, often every three days. After a bout of malaria, I'm exhausted and I need several days to even be able to stand up again.

Tex A. Snap

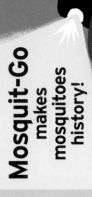

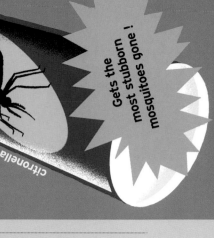

In 1897, Ronald Ross, an English doctor in India, proved that it was the anopheles mosquito that spread the parasite. The puzzle was solved. When a female mosquito bites a person who has malaria, it absorbs the parasite that is in his or her blood. Then, when it bites another person, the parasite is passed on, and he or she gets sick, too.

In the 1950s, a worldwide effort against malaria was launched. Swamps were drained and a powerful insecticide used. But the insecticide had harmful effects on the environment and hasn't been used for 30 years. Mosquitoes have become more resistant, and medicines less effective. For the last 10 years, the focus has been on research.

Tex A. Snap

Malaria Across the World   by Claire Itty

The green areas are affected by malaria.

Each year, malaria kills between 1.5 million and 2.7 million people. Nine out of 10 cases occur in Africa, but the illness is making a comeback in India and other Asian countries. There are between 300 million and 500 million people who suffer from it.

News Briefs

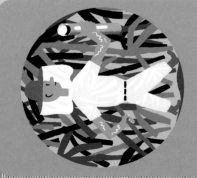

How Travelers Can Take Precautions

Wear light, loose clothing that covers you from head to toe. Use anti-mosquito bug-sprays or lotions. Take preventative medicine. These are the steps a traveler needs to take when visiting areas where there is a risk of malaria.

2002: A Historic Year!

In 2002, scientists mapped the genes of the anopheles mosquito, the plasmodium (the parasite that carries the illness), and humans. This raised hopes that we will be able to fight the mosquito better, make medicines that will kill the parasite, or create vaccines to protect people.

Ed Shorter

Then and Now

When they came to the Americas in the 16th century, the Spanish conquistadors launched a hunt for El Dorado, a man of legend who was supposedly covered in gold, and who lived in a fabulous city made of gold. The conquistadors searched in Colombia, Venezuela, and Guyana. But they had no luck—no El Dorado, no golden city. So they resorted to pillaging the villages they traveled through. El Dorado was a myth, but the robbing was unfortunately real.

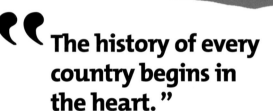

Have you ever heard of a machine that can take you through time, traveling back into the past and forward into the future? You'll find a machine just like that in the pages of a novel called *The Time Machine*, written way back in 1895 by Herbert George Wells. If you're ready to go to the year 802701, hang on tight to the book jacket and take off!

" The history of every country begins in the heart. "

Willa Cather (1873–1947)

It is written: "Death shall come on swift wings to him who disturbs the sleep of the king." But that didn't stop archeologist Howard Carter and his team from celebrating when, on November 4, 1922, they discovered the tomb of the Egyptian boy–king Tutankhamen. They paid no attention to the hieroglyphs over the entrance to the crypt. Coincidence? Curse? In the following years, 17 scientists from the expedition lost their lives under circumstances some say were suspicious.

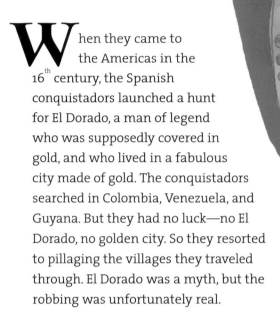

Our History

Time goes by, generations succeed each other, as do legends, cultures, wars, and leaders. What purpose does history serve? Maybe to help us see what we owe to those who came before us, and to find our place in the long chain of humanity.

Legend has it that thousands of years ago, the people of the island of Atlantis angered the gods, who drowned the island and all its inhabitants. Today, there are still researchers and adventurers who scour ancient texts and legends with a magnifying glass hoping to find a clue that will lead them to find the Lost Continent. They don't all agree about where it is. Some of them think it is under the Atlantic Ocean, others that it's beneath the Mediterranean. There are even a few who are searching in the sand dunes of the Sahara!

Prehistory

The earliest people are said to have lived 6 million years ago, on the continent of Africa. That's the beginning of "prehistory," a period that lasted millions of years until the invention of script.

Humans and monkeys have common ancestors. About 6 or 7 million years ago, those ancestors split along two separate lines: the humans and the monkeys. The first humans still looked like the great apes. They evolved slowly and went through several stages before becoming humans like us.

About 3.5 million years ago

Australopithecus is one of our distant ancestors. He doesn't make tools but he walks upright without the aid of his hands.

Traces of our ancestors...

The **Tournai skull** is 6 or 7 million years old.

The skeleton of **Lucy**, an *australopithecus*, dates back 3.1 million years.

The **oldest tool** is this pebble shaped by *homo habilis*.

A flint, sharp on **both sides**, was carved by *homo erectus*.

Painted cave walls in Altamira, Spain, show painted animals and the hunt.

About 2.6 million years ago

Homo habilis is the first human. He can make tools and build huts out of branches.

About 2 million years ago

Homo erectus learns to make fire. He uses it to cook food, provide warmth, light up the cave, keep animals away, and harden the tip of his spear to be able to hunt better.

About 200,000 years ago

Neanderthal man is the first to bury the dead. He uses carved flints to hunt big game.

About 40,000 years ago

Homo sapiens is modern man, like us. He knows how to sculpt statues, make jewelry, and paint animals on the walls of a cave.

A clay **Venus** figurine, among the oldest ceramics in the world.

A long time ago, all people were nomadic. They went from place to place in search of something to eat—animals to hunt, fruit, and other wild foods to gather. It took thousands of years for our ancestors to learn how to produce their own food by farming and raising animals. Since they needed to be near their fields to grow crops, they built the first villages and settled down.

The Egyptians

timeline

About 3100 B.C.E.
The reign of Narmer, the first pharaoh.

About 2600 B.C.E.
The pharaoh Cheops builds the tallest pyramid.

About 1340 B.C.E.
Death of the pharaoh Tutankhamen.

About 1290 B.C.E.
Beginning of the long reign of the pharaoh Ramses II.

332 B.C.E.
Alexander the Great of Greece conquers Egypt.

For 3,000 years, the powerful pharaohs of Egypt ruled from the banks of the Nile. Their people built enormous monuments, invented an early form of writing, and worshipped mysterious gods.

It is 1343 B.C.E. The boy pharaoh Tutankhamen has just died. A long procession accompanies the body of the dead king towards his tomb where, according to Egyptian beliefs, he will begin his journey to the Afterworld.

The **funeral barge** is a symbol of the journey to the land of the dead.

Anubis, god of the dead, is carried along.

The **coffin** contains the pharaoh's mummy.

Slaves carry everything the pharaoh could need in the Afterlife: furniture, jewelry, food…

Egypt of the Pharaohs

Mediterranean Sea

PORT OF ALEXANDRIA

Pyramids of Giza

Red Sea

Nile River

LUXOR

ABU SIMBEL TEMPLE

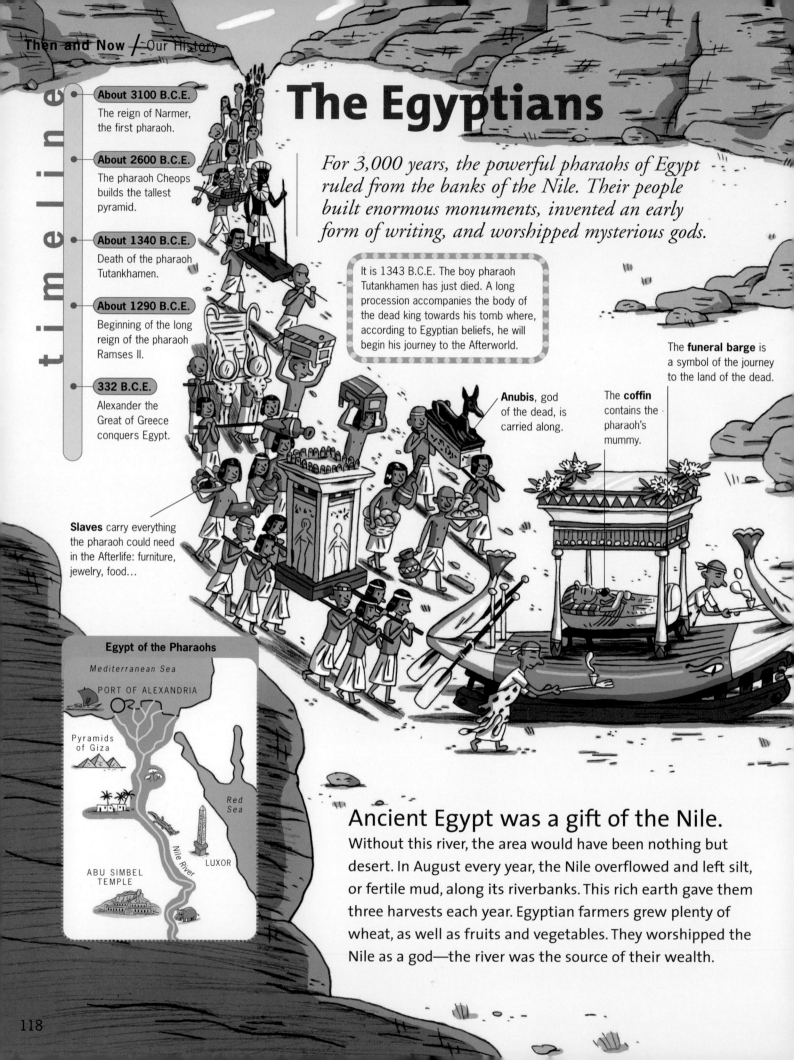

Ancient Egypt was a gift of the Nile.

Without this river, the area would have been nothing but desert. In August every year, the Nile overflowed and left silt, or fertile mud, along its riverbanks. This rich earth gave them three harvests each year. Egyptian farmers grew plenty of wheat, as well as fruits and vegetables. They worshipped the Nile as a god—the river was the source of their wealth.

Many pharaohs' tombs were built in the **Valley of the Kings**.

The entrance to the **tomb** is carved out of rock.

Sacred texts are written on the walls. They are made up of **hieroglyphs**, the characters Egyptians use for writing.

The mummy lies inside three coffins.

The paintings depict **the gods** and the pharoah's life after his death.

Official mourners weep and gesture to express everyone's grief.

Priests lead the procession.

The **family and entourage** of the pharaoh go first.

Two carved **sentries** guard the inner tomb.

The **antechamber** is full of things that belonged to the pharaoh.

The pharaoh reigned over all his subjects with absolute power. He was considered a living god, the son of Ra, the sun god. He had a prime minister to help govern, and was surrounded by courtiers in his grand palace. Priests and bureaucrats were also part of high society. The rest of the population was made up of craftsmen, farmers, and slaves.

It's 1922, 3,379 years later. An archeologist has just discovered Tutankhamen's tomb…

119

Those Brilliant Greeks!

Around 2,500 years ago, a small nation on the Mediterranean Sea called Greece built a sophisticated civilization. The Greeks developed so much: philosophy, democracy, and competitive sports....

Timeline

About 776 B.C.E.
First Olympic Games.

About 700 B.C.E.
Greeks spread out to the Mediterranean coast.

507 B.C.E.
The city of Athens becomes a democracy.

About 480 B.C.E.
Start of the classical age: the height of Greek culture.

447 B.C.E.
The Parthenon is built in Athens.

323 B.C.E.
Death of Alexander the Great, conqueror of lands as far away as India.

4 Actors wore masks to represent their characters.

Number Crunch

3 is the number of baths a Greek person took daily.

7.5 m (over 24 ft.) is the record for the long jump, set by Kyonis in the 7th century B.C.E., and still unbeaten.

330,000 is how many people lived in Athens in the 5th century B.C.E.

18,000 km (11,185 miles) is the distance Alexander the Great traveled over 11 years.

1 Architects built temples with perfect proportions to honor the gods.

*The largest Greek temple is **the Parthenon** in Athens.*

2 The Greeks were unbeatable in **geometry** and **calculus.** They figured out how to measure the Earth's width.

*Brillant thinkers were **Thales, Pythagoras,** and **Archimedes.***

3 Poets wrote wonderful mythological tales of both legend and truth. They invented tragedy and comedy in the theater.

*The **Iliad,** by **Homer,** is a famous poem about ancient wars and gods.*

5 Philosophers tried to find answers to the big questions of life.

*Important philosophers were **Socrates**, **Plato**, **Aristotle**, and **Epicurus.***

A Greek child's **doll**.

A **coin**.

Ulysses, hero of the *Iliad* and the *Odyssey*, painted on a vase.

Greek Colonies

Marseilles
Ampurias
Naples
GREECE
Byzantium
Black Sea
Sinope
Heracles
Rhegion
Athens
Phocea
Carthage
Syracuse
Miletus
Cyrene
Mediterranean Sea

8 The Greeks believed in **gods** that looked like people.

Athena was the goddess of war.

11 Historians traveled and found witnesses to report on what had happened in the past.

The first historian was **Herodotus.**

12 The Greeks were **great sailors.** They knew how to navigate, and they reached cities all around the Mediterranean.

Piraeus was the main port of Athens.

10 The Greeks turned **medicine** into a science.

Hippocrates *was a great doctor.*

9 Greek soldiers trained hard and became **fierce warriors.**

The Spartans from the city of Sparta were famous soldiers.

6 The Greeks invented **democracy.** They were the first to vote on laws and elect their leaders.

A famous politician and orator was **Pericles.**

7 Sculptors created beautiful statues.

Phidias *was a talented sculptor.*

The Olympic Games were held in honor of Zeus, king of the gods, every four years in the town of Olympus. While the games were on, the various cities stopped all their wars. Foot races, boxing, long jump, and discus and javelin throwing all took place in the stadium. Athletes often competed without clothing—both because the weather was very hot and also in celebration of their fine human form. The hippodrome was where chariots raced. Winners got a simple crown of laurel leaves, but their glory spread throughout Greece.

Timeline

753 B.C.E
Rome is founded by Romulus and Remus.

509 B.C.E.
Rome goes from being a kingdom to being a republic.

265 B.C.E.
The Romans conquer all of Italy.

44 B.C.E.
Julius Caesar is assassinated.

27 B.C.E.
Augustus becomes the first Roman Emperor.

0

476
The end of the Roman Empire.

Caesar in his chariot. He is seen to be all-powerful, like a living god.

The Forum is surrounded by government **buildings and temples** of white marble.

An eagle is the symbol of the empire.

A tribal chieftan, conquered by Caesar.

Rome

A small, sheep-herding village called Rome, in Italy, grew over several centuries into the largest empire of the ancient world. Roman civilization lasted six hundred years. And traces of it remain throughout Europe, North Africa, and the Middle East.

In 753 B.C.E., the legend goes, two brothers named Romulus and Remus founded the city of Rome. They had been abandoned at birth, but a mother wolf found them and nursed them like cubs. Rome was ruled by kings for two centuries as it grew. But in 509 B.C.E., there was a revolt and the kings were thrown out. Rome became a republic, where power belonged to its people.

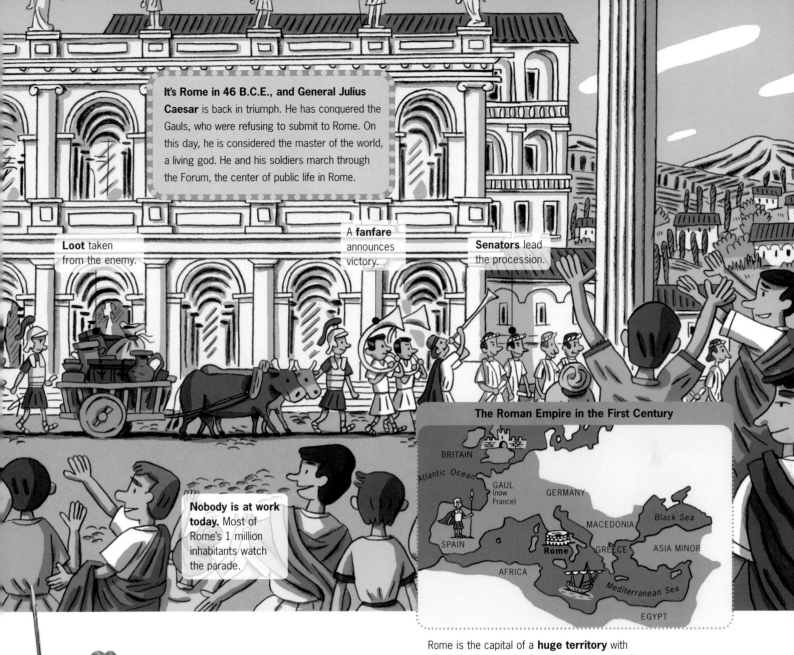

It's Rome in 46 B.C.E., and General Julius Caesar is back in triumph. He has conquered the Gauls, who were refusing to submit to Rome. On this day, he is considered the master of the world, a living god. He and his soldiers march through the Forum, the center of public life in Rome.

Loot taken from the enemy.

A **fanfare** announces victory.

Senators lead the procession.

Nobody is at work today. Most of Rome's 1 million inhabitants watch the parade.

The Roman Empire in the First Century

BRITAIN

Atlantic Ocean

GAUL (now France)

GERMANY

SPAIN

Rome

MACEDONIA

Black Sea

GREECE

ASIA MINOR

AFRICA

Mediterranean Sea

EGYPT

Rome is the capital of a **huge territory** with 70 million inhabitants. Soldiers and slaves built roads that made it easy to get around the empire.

The Romans were unbeatable! Their secret was their army. While Rome's enemies used mostly mercenaries*, the Roman army was made up of citizens who fought to defend their own country. A legion was made up of 6,000 men, and all citizens between the ages of 17 and 45 had to serve. The legionnaires followed strict discipline. Being well organized made it easier for them to conquer others.

An immense empire covered the whole Mediterranean basin and Asia Minor. Julius Caesar, Rome's most famous general, had conquered Gaul. His nephew, Augustus, became the first Roman Emperor. Rome's borders would soon spread from Scotland to Arabia. For more than two centuries, the Empire would experience outstanding peace and prosperity. But in the 5th century, Barbarians from the east forced their way into the Roman interior.

* Soldiers who fight for any army in exchange for money.

KNOW-IT-ALL NEWS

Vera Smart
Editor-in-chief

Ashley Asks
Interviewer

Tex A. Snap
Photo Journalist

Claire Itty
Researcher

Art Phul
Illustrator

Ed Shorter
News Briefs

From the Editor's Desk

To celebrate Rome's great military victories, the Emperor has given Romans four months of free spectacular events. There's a full program of chariot races, gladiator fights, and ferocious beasts.

Vera Smart

Art Phul

Let the Games Begin!

There's an amazing event taking place on the first day of the games: a re-enactment of the naval battle of Salamis from six centuries ago. The stadium has been flooded with water, and two battle ships make a grand entrance. On board are gladiators dressed in costumes of the era. It's Greek warriors against Persian warriors! Flaming arrows are fired, there's hand-to-hand combat with daggers. The fighting is bloody and there are many dead. The spectators are loving it!

Schedule of today's events:

- 10:00 a.m. African Animal Hunt
- 2:00 p.m. Chariot Races, with Diocles
- 7:00 p.m. The Emperor's Buffet, open to all Romans

Ashley met writer Pliny the Younger. He gave her his opinion of the games.

Like thousands of other Romans, do you have your place reserved at the games?
Absolutely not! I would rather leave Rome. This sort of entertainment annoys me greatly.

Don't you have the least bit of interest in how good the fighters are?
You know, the fighters don't have to be any good to draw a crowd. People come to cheer on their favorite, no matter how good he is. If he changes the color of his tunic, the public will pick another favorite. The whole thing makes people act stupid.

You don't think much of how people have fun...
That's true. Romans can do whatever they want with their time. They love to see blood flow. I'd rather write on my tablets far away from all the nasty cheering.

The fights are the favorite of bloodthirsty Romans. Yesterday, the audience had no pity. They only raised their thumbs up twice. That's the signal to the winner to spare the life of the loser.

A battle between wild animals features a rhinoceros and tigers. It's estimated that 50,000 animals will be slaughtered during the four months of the games.　　**Tex A. Snap**

At 9:30 a.m., trumpets sound the official opening of the games. All kinds of gladiators march into the arena. There are fierce Thracians, and Mirmillones armed with daggers. There are Retiarii, carrying nets to capture their opponents. There are Velites bearing lances. But all eyes are on the imperial grandstand to catch a glimpse of the Emperor. As the gladiators parade in front of him, they offer the traditional greeting: "Hail Caesar! We who are about to die salute you!" Many of them won't live to see the sun set.

Muscularus

Muscularus can transform...

SLAVES...

CRIMINALS...

BEGGARS...

THIEVES...

...INTO HEROES OF THE ARENA!

The Top Gladiator School

14,000 Gladiators

will face off over the four months. Most of them are prisoners of war who have been sold to rich Romans as slaves. Their masters send them for special fight training. When the masters decide the gladiators are ready, they throw them into the stadium. Very few get out alive.

A Ray of Hope

If a gladiator wins several times, he might be able to stop fighting and become a trainer at a gladiator school.

Ed Shorter

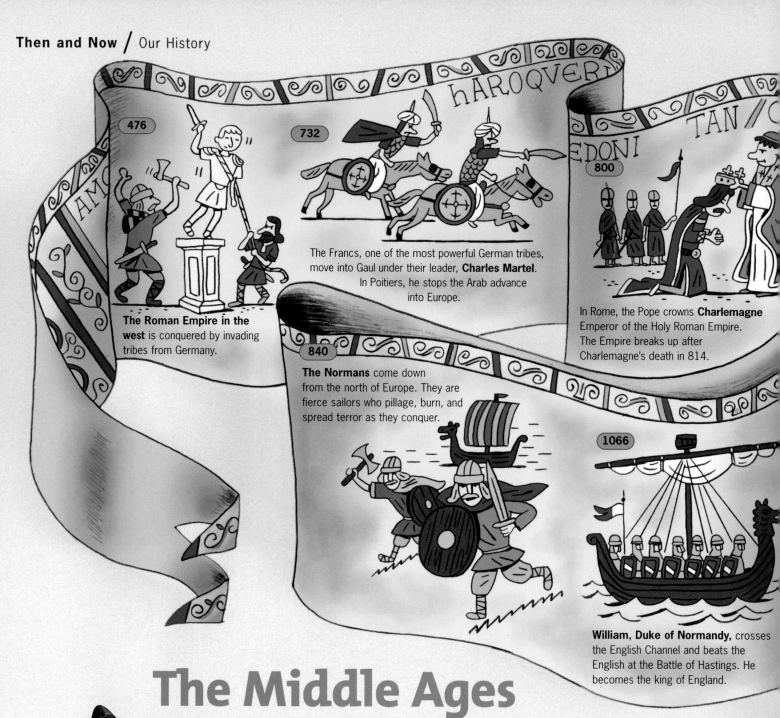

476 The Roman Empire in the west is conquered by invading tribes from Germany.

732 The Francs, one of the most powerful German tribes, move into Gaul under their leader, **Charles Martel**. In Poitiers, he stops the Arab advance into Europe.

800 In Rome, the Pope crowns **Charlemagne** Emperor of the Holy Roman Empire. The Empire breaks up after Charlemagne's death in 814.

840 **The Normans** come down from the north of Europe. They are fierce sailors who pillage, burn, and spread terror as they conquer.

1066 **William, Duke of Normandy,** crosses the English Channel and beats the English at the Battle of Hastings. He becomes the king of England.

The Middle Ages

The period we call the "Middle Ages" lasted for a thousand years. It began with the end of the Roman Empire in the 5th century, and lasted until the discovery of America in the 15th century.

Knights, protected by heavy armor, fought on horseback.

It was a violent era in Europe, with many wars and invasions. There was no single, organized government. Each lord in his castle defended his territory. People "belonged" to the lord under the feudal regime. By the 12th century, strong kings, like Philip II Augustus in France, and Richard I the Lionheart in England imposed their authority on their countries and created more ordered societies.

The only strong and stable power during these troubled times was the **Christian church**. After the end of the Roman Empire, Europe's inhabitants gradually converted to Christianity. The head of the church was the pope. He was in charge of priests and bishops who were responsible for leading and organizing the faithful. Daily life became centered on religion. All day long, church clocks would chime the hours for prayer, and the year would be marked by religious festivals.

Just like the pages of a book, **stained glass windows** in cathedrals told religious stories.

1271–1291

The great voyager **Marco Polo** takes a long trip across Asia. He goes as far as China. He brings back things Europeans had never seen: pepper, cinnamon, tea, and porcelain.

12ᵗʰ century

Huge, tall churches are built. These are the **first cathedrals.**

1337–1453

The kings of England and France go to war. The **100 Years War** was the longest fight of the Middle Ages.

1096–1270

The Muslim Turks try to stop Christian pilgrimages to Jerusalem. The pope urges Christians to liberate the Holy Land. This was the first **Crusade.**

1338–1351

The **Plague!** It was a terrible epidemic that killed one third of the population of Europe and Asia.

1429

Joan of Arc leads the French army to force the English out of France.

Life in the Middle Ages

Society in Europe during the Middle Ages was made up of three types: those who prayed (priests, monks), those who fought (knights), and those who worked (farmers, townspeople).

By the 11th century, tribes have **stopped invading each other's lands**, which makes the roads safer for trading goods. Cities grow and become richer as commerce spreads.

Town **streets** are narrow and dirty, and have no pavement or gutters. Stagnant water allows germs to breed. Plague epidemics kill millions of people.

On market days, peasants come into the town to sell their goods.

Monks live as a community in a **monastery.** They pray for the wellbeing of others, as well as work their own land. They work the fields, grow vegetables, keep animals, and welcome pilgrims.

The **castle** is the lord's stronghold against his enemies. A few hundred guards can keep a whole army outside the fortified walls.

Peasants work the lord's lands. They give him half of their harvest and work for free several days a week in the castle. This is "indentured servitude."

The **lord** is the absolute master of his lands. But he is responsible for the safety and wellbeing of the peasants in his domain.

The Renaissance

The Renaissance was a period when the arts and knowledge flowered and flourished. It began in Italian cities in the 15th century.

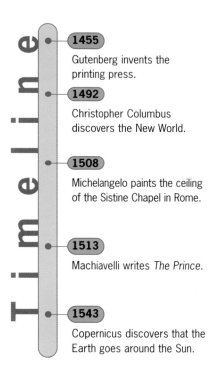

Timeline

1455
Gutenberg invents the printing press.

1492
Christopher Columbus discovers the New World.

1508
Michelangelo paints the ceiling of the Sistine Chapel in Rome.

1513
Machiavelli writes *The Prince*.

1543
Copernicus discovers that the Earth goes around the Sun.

In Venice, Florence, and Rome, and then throughout Europe, there was a renewed passion for the ideas and arts of the Ancient World. And in this "rebirth" of classical ideas, new ideas were born. Painters, architects, and writers became famous, and princes became their admirers and protectors. Artists like Michelangelo and Leonard da Vinci created masterpieces. Thanks to the printing press, there were more books, and they could be made more cheaply, so ideas were able to spread throughout society.

Spotlight on...

Leonardo da Vinci

Born: in 1452, in Vinci, near Florence.
Profession: "Renaissance man" (painter, sculptor, architect, engineer, philosopher, and inventor).
Addresses: in Florence, Milan, and Rome, Italy. Then with the King of France.
Works: *The Mona Lisa*, flying machines, the assault tank, among other things.
Died: 1519, in France.

Florence, around 1490...

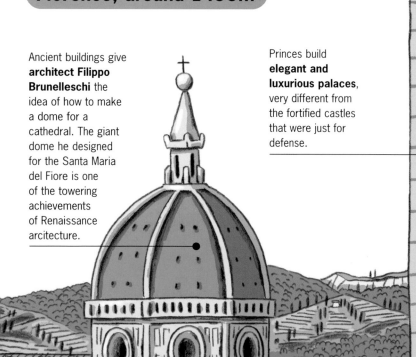

Ancient buildings give **architect Filippo Brunelleschi** the idea of how to make a dome for a cathedral. The giant dome he designed for the Santa Maria del Fiore is one of the towering achievements of Renaissance arcitecture.

Princes build **elegant and luxurious palaces,** very different from the fortified castles that were just for defense.

20 million books are printed in the second half of the 15th century.

Windows are much larger than they were in castles, and they let light in.

Prince Lorenzo the Magnificent is a member of the powerful Medici family. He likes to surround himself with artists and thinkers. This evening, he is having a dinner for some famous ones.

Painters play with light and color, and know how to show perspective.

Lorenzo the Magnificent

Michelangelo is still quite young, but the prince recognizes his talent.

Sandro Botticelli, painter of *The Birth of Venus*.

Leonardo da Vinci

Mirrors, marble, and gold decorate the walls.

Christopher Columbus will soon discover America. Magellan is going around the world.

A portable timepiece.

The table is beautifully set, with porcelain and Venetian glass.

Pico della Mirandola writes: "There is nothing more admirable than man." He believes that human perfection is possible.

No more eating with fingers! There are **forks!**

131

The New World

After Christopher Columbus found out what lay on the western side of the Atlantic, European nations didn't waste any time sending explorers, armies, and settlers to lay claim to the riches of the "Americas."

Acadian flag

Britain sent John Cabot, who

landed in and named Newfoundland. France sent Samuel de Champlain, who mapped out what is now Quebec. Portugal sent Pedro Alvares Cabral, who claimed Brazil for the Portuguese crown. And Spain sent Hernán Cortés, who brought down the Aztec Empire in what today is Mexico.

John Cabot

The French who settled Newfoundland, New Brunswick, Prince Edward Island, and Nova Scotia in the 1600s became known as the **Acadians**.

French explorer **Jacques Cartier** was the first to use the name Canada, in 1535. It comes from the word "kanata" in the Huron-Iroquois language, meaning "village or settlement." Cartier used it to refer to the village of Stadacona (Quebec City today) and surrounding area.

Etienne Brûlé was a French scout who traveled with the native people of what is now Ontario, and got to know them.

William Penn, an English Quaker, created the Commonwealth of Pennsylvania in 1681, the first settlement to have a written constitution and to promote religious tolerance.

The Plymouth Plantation in Massachusetts was where the English Puritans first celebrated Thanksgiving in 1621.

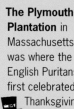

Dutchman Peter Minuit traded 24 dollars worth of beads and trinkets for the Island of Manhattan, which he named New Amsterdam, in 1626. The English renamed it New York in 1664.

The most successful of the early English settlements was at **Jamestown, Virginia**, in 1607.

Canada today

USA today

Mexico Today

Spotlight on...

Pocahontas

"Pocahontas" means "naughty child" in Algonquian. It was a nickname given to Matoaka, the daughter of Chief Powhatan, who ruled a large area of what is now Virginia. The little girl befriended Captain John Smith at the English colony established in 1607 in Jamestown. Smith said that Pocahontas saved his life when she was only 10. But then, relations between the Powhatan nation and the English deteriorated and Pocahontas was kidnapped and held for ransom. When her tribe paid only a part, Pocahontas stayed with the English. She married a planter named John Rolfe and changed her name to Rebecca. She went to England where she met the Queen and became a sensation. Sadly, she died on the trip home.

Native Americans introduced the Europeans to...

Can you imagine a world without chocolate, corn, or potatoes? Native Americans, who'd lived in these lands for thousands of years, were the first to cultivate many kinds of food crops, grown all over the world today. Europeans brought these crops back from the Americas and they helped to reduce hunger and disease in Europe. Native healers also developed pain medicines and other pharmaceuticals centuries ago that have helped to form our modern-day concepts of medicine.

These everyday foods and other items were introduced to Europeans by Native Americans:

turkey · tomato · potato · sweet potato · avocado · chocolate

vanilla · chili peppers · pecan nuts · rubber · chewing gum · cotton

timeline

10000 B.C.E.
Founding of Haida Gwai ("Our Land"), by the Haida First Nation in what is now the Queen Charlotte Islands, British Columbia.

2000 B.C.E.
The Hohokam people build a city in what today is Tucson, Arizona.

1000
Vikings led by Leif Ericson arrive in what is now Newfoundland, Canada, and establish a settlement called Vinland.

250–900
Classic period of the Mayan Empire in Central America.

1492
Christopher Columbus lands in what is now Haiti.

1541
Basque fishermen from Spain set up a port in Newfoundland and call it San Juan (later St. John's).

1565
The Spanish build a town called St. Augustine in what is now Florida.

1586
Sir Walter Raleigh tries—and fails—to establish a colony at Roanoke, Virginia.

1599
François Gravé Du Pont and Pierre Chauvin de Tonnetuit set up a fur-trading post at the mouth of the Saguenay River in present-day Quebec.

1605
Frenchman Pierre Dugua, the Sieur des Monts, founds Port Royal (now Annapolis) in Nova Scotia.

Sept. 6, 1620
The *Mayflower* sails from England to found the Plymouth Colony in today's Massachusetts.

The Industrial Revolution

A Century of Inventions

1769
James Watt invents the steam engine.
James Watt

1800
Locomotive invented.

1819
Steamboat invented.

1827
Nicéphore Niépce invents photography.
N. Niépce

1871
Electricity invented.

1876
Alexander Graham Bell invents the telephone.
Graham Bell

1877
Phonograph invented by Thomas Edison.

1879
Thomas Edison invents the light bulb.
Thomas Edison

1885
Louis Pasteur invents a vaccine against rabies.

1886
Gasoline-fueled car invented.

1895
The Lumière Brothers invent movies.
Louis Pasteur

1897
First flight of an airplane with a motor.

In the 19th century, transport, industry, and cities themselves grew, thanks to new technologies. These changes transformed peoples' lives.

The steam engine was the most important invention of the industrial revolution. It was used to make machines in factories, as well as locomotives and steamboats. For centuries, going on foot or by horse were the only ways of getting around. These new forms of transportation made traveling quicker, and made distances seem shorter.

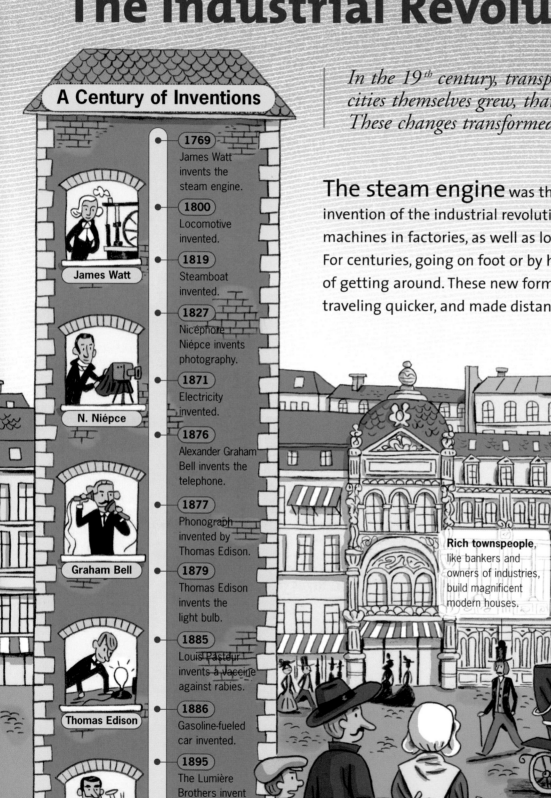

Rich townspeople, like bankers and owners of industries, build magnificent modern houses.

People flock to the city from the countryside. The city of Liverpool, in England, grows 5 times as large in 50 years.

First there are steam-driven cars, then ones that run on **gasoline**.

New industries hired lots of workers. Many were farmers or craftsmen without work. They left the countryside to live in the city, closer to the factories and the mines. Many others left Europe for newer cities like New York and Montreal. The population of cities grew. From that point on, London and Paris never had fewer than 1 million inhabitants, and North American cities grew even bigger.

The great changes of the 19th century inspired the writer **Jules Verne** to dream up even more amazing inventions in his books.

Why did children have to work?

Wages paid to workers were so low that a family couldn't survive on them. The only way to feed an entire family was if everyone worked. Parents sent their children, both boys and girls as young as six or seven, to work in the factories or in the mines for 12 or even 14 hours a day.

The first **airplanes** fly only 30 m (less than 100 ft.).

Industry produces **iron and steel**, which is used to build bridges, railway tracks, and train stations.

The **train** links major cities. A trip that previously took a week by carriage now takes only a day!

Steamboats cross the Atlantic from Europe to New York in only 10 days.

Working families live in poor housing next to the factories and mines.

A **small child** can work in the narrowest tunnels of the coal mines.

Miners need to go **deep underground** into the mines to find coal.

Some tunnels are **too narrow** for an adult to stand up in.

Steam engines run on **coal**, which has to be dug up in mines.

The First World War

Timeline

28 June 1914
Archduke Franz Ferdinand of Austria is assassinated in Sarajevo. Austria declares war on Serbia.

1 August 1914
Russia, France, and Germany prepare their armies for war. Germany declares war on Russia, then France two days later.

4 August 1914
Germany invades Belgium. Great Britain, including Canada, enters war in Belgium's defense.

February to December 1916
500,000 soldiers are killed at the Battle of Verdun.

2 April 1917
U.S.A. enters war.

11 November 1918
War ends. Ten million people are dead; millions more wounded.

In 1914, tensions between several European nations exploded into a full-scale war. The battles were fiercer than any ever known before.

A soldier wearing a gas mask.

They fought on land, at sea and—for the first time ever—in the sky. Airplanes were used to drop bombs on the enemy. Fearsome new weapons were introduced: poison gas, tanks, and machine guns. But neither side was able to come out on top. The front lines became fixed, and the armies stood in trenches dug into the earth and topped with barbed wire, facing each other. The soldiers suffered horribly. Every assault was useless, killing and injuring hundreds at a time.

Between 1914 and 1918, millions of families are split apart as sons and fathers go off to war.

Saying goodbye on railway platforms, mothers, wives, and sweethearts hope that the "war to end all wars" will soon be over and their loved ones will return home safely.

140

Trenches built below ground level are freezing cold and full of mud. Soldiers hide in them between battles and some pass the time by writing letters home.

tune in

The Wild Poppies

On May 15, 1915, **Lieutenant Colonel John McCrae** of the Canadian Army helped bury a friend killed in the Second Battle of Ypres, Belgium. He noticed the beautiful red wild-flowers between the graves, and the next day he wrote a poem that has forever linked poppies to the remembrance of fallen soldiers. The now famous poem begins with the moving lines: "In Flanders fields the poppies blow between the crosses, row on row..."

Machine guns and cannons fire all around, letting the soldiers know that the battle is on. The commander orders a charge. Armed with bayonets, the soldiers leave the trenches and hurl themselves toward enemy lines through a hail of bullets.

The guns fall silent on November 11, 1918 with the surrender of Germany. Peace at last! News arrives that soldiers will return home. Six months later, the Treaty of Versailles creates a new Europe. Gone is the Austro-Hungarian Empire that had ruled most of eastern Europe. Now countries like Poland and Czechoslovakia will have self-government.

November 11 is the day we honor those who fought to preserve democracy. In many countries, people wear poppies to say, "I remember."

The Second World War

1939: war rips the world apart once more. It is one of the worst events in human history: concentration camps, bombings, and atomic weapons claimed millions of victims around the world.

1933
Hitler is elected Chancellor of Germany.

1 September 1939
Germany invades Poland.

3–10 September 1939
Britain, France, Australia, New Zealand, and Canada declare war on Germany.

The German army marches into Paris; 8 days later, France surrenders.

14 June 1940

27 September 1940
Germany, Italy, and Japan become allies and form the Axis.

The Japanese bomb U.S. ships in Pearl Harbor, Hawaii.

7 December 1941

2 February 1943
Russia defeats the Germans at Stalingrad; it's the first German loss.

1944
The British, Canadians, and Americans land in Normandy to liberate France.

Germany surrenders. British, American, and Russian leaders meet at Yalta to plan the future of the world.

8 May 1945

Adolf Hitler, leader of the Nazi Party, and Germany's Chancellor, thought his country should be the most powerful one in the world. He claimed that the Germans are descended from a superior race and that gave them the right to dominate other people. His ideas led to a dictatorship in Germany and a world war. In 1939, the German army invaded several European countries. The only nation to stand up to Hitler was Great Britain.

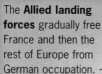

The **Allied landing forces** gradually free France and then the rest of Europe from German occupation.

In April 1945, the German capital **Berlin** is surrounded by the Russians and the Americans. On April 30, Hitler commits suicide in his bunker.

In August 1944, the Allies land in Paris. On the streets of the city, American soldiers replace German ones. The people are happy to live in a **free country** again.

In 1941, the Americans and Russians joined the war against Germany. A few months later, Germany's ally, Japan, attacked the United States in the Pacific. The war became truly global—there was fighting almost everywhere on the planet. Aerial bombardments destroyed entire cities and killed many of their inhabitants. In six years of war, 52 million people were killed. It was the most murderous war in history.

Anne Frank

Born: June 12, 1929, in Germany. **Her life:** Anne was Jewish. Her parents fled Hitler's Germany and the family settled in Holland. When the Germans invaded Holland, Anne and her family hid in an attic. For two years, the young girl kept a journal. She wrote of her life, her fears, her dreams, and her joys. The journal ends on August 1, 1944. Three days later, she and her whole family were discovered, arrested, and deported to a concentration camp. **Her death:** in March, 1945, in the camp at Bergen–Belsen. *The Diary of Anne Frank* was published around the world following her death. You can still read it today.

In 1945, there is ruin everywhere. Europe is freed from German occupation, but the war between the Americans and Japanese rages on. And that year, the world faces two great traumas: the discovery of the Nazi death camps, and detonation of the atomic bomb—the most powerful weapon ever.

Eastern Europe is nothing but rubble. Entire cities have been wiped out and the human toll is beyond belief. Russia has lost 10% of its population. One-quarter of all Poles have been killed by bombs, persecution, famine, or in battle.

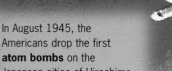

In August 1945, the Americans drop the first **atom bombs** on the Japanese cities of Hiroshima and Nagasaki. One hundred thousand people die, and thousands more get radiation sickness. The Japanese surrender.

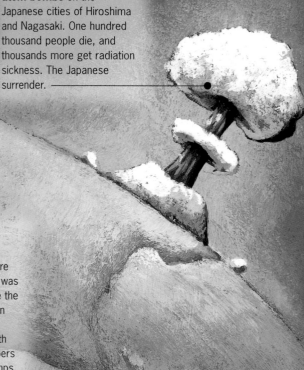

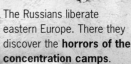

The Russians liberate eastern Europe. There they discover the **horrors of the concentration camps**.

The **Nazis murdered millions of people** who stood up to them, or were of a race the Nazis said was "inferior." The Jews were the primary target. Six million Jews died—imprisoned, tortured, and put to death in the poison gas chambers of the concentration camps.

The World Since 1945

After two world wars, Europe was divided into West and East, with the countries of the East under the control of the communist Soviet Union. The Soviet Union and the United States faced off in the "Cold War." Amazing scientific discoveries made life much better for many. But dictatorships and massacres continued....

1948

On May 14, the Jewish National Council announces the birth of the **state of Israel.** The next day, Arab troops enter the former Palestine. The **first Arab–Israeli War** begins.

1949

Mao Ze Dong's Revolutionary Army enters Peking, China's capital, in triumph. Mao announces the creation of the People's Republic of China, a communist country.

1947

One by one, countries that have been colonized by Europe declare their independence. India's leader, **Gandhi,** uses a philosophy of **non-violence** to win his country's freedom from Great Britain.

1957

Germany, France, Italy, Belgium, Holland, and Luxemburg sign the Treaty of Rome. The **European Economic Community** is created.

1961

The Soviet *Vostok I* rocket is launched, carrying cosmonaut Yuri Gagarin, the **first man in space.**

1969

Man walks on the Moon! American astronaut Neil Armstrong is the first human visitor on the Moon. He lands on the Sea of Tranquility.

1973

During the 4th Arab–Israeli war, the Arab countries in the Organization of Petrol Exporting Countries (OPEC) raise the price of oil very sharply. It causes a serious global economic crisis. This is the first **oil shock.**

1979

The **Islamic Revolution** takes over Iran. The Shah, or emperor, of Iran flees. The ayatollah Khomeini returns from exile to become the country's leader. Islamist movements grow all over the Arab world.

1989

The wall dividing the city of Berlin that was built during the Cold War comes tumbling down. It's the end of the **Cold War and communism in Europe**. The following year, East and West Germany re-unite as one nation.

1990

Saddam Hussein, the Iraqi dictator, invades Kuwait. President George Bush of the United States and several European countries declare war on Iraq.

1994

A civil war breaks out between the Hutu and Tutsi tribes of Rwanda, a small country in central Africa. The Hutu try to exterminate the Tutsi. Half a million Tutsi are massacred. It's a **genocide.**

2001

Two airplanes crash into the **World Trade Center in New York**. The attack is organized by terrorist Osama bin Laden. In 2003, President George W. Bush uses the attack as justification for a new war against Iraq, and topples Saddam Hussein.

"

You are lost if you forget
that the fruits belong to all
and that the Earth belongs
to no one."

Jean-Jacques Rousseau (1712–1778)

No more overpopulation, misery, and loneliness. Imagine an island with 54 towns exactly the same, each town made up of 6,000 families, and each family having no more than 30 members. Everyone eats together, all belongings are shared, and no one works more than six hours a day. This is Utopia, an ideal society imagined by Thomas More in his book called *Utopia*, published in 1516. Do you think you'd like to live there?

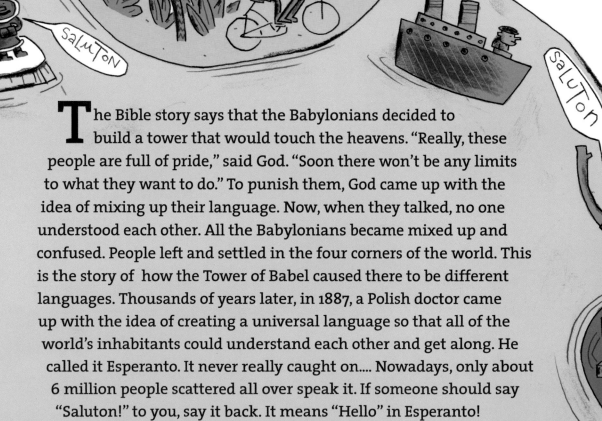

The Bible story says that the Babylonians decided to build a tower that would touch the heavens. "Really, these people are full of pride," said God. "Soon there won't be any limits to what they want to do." To punish them, God came up with the idea of mixing up their language. Now, when they talked, no one understood each other. All the Babylonians became mixed up and confused. People left and settled in the four corners of the world. This is the story of how the Tower of Babel caused there to be different languages. Thousands of years later, in 1887, a Polish doctor came up with the idea of creating a universal language so that all of the world's inhabitants could understand each other and get along. He called it Esperanto. It never really caught on.... Nowadays, only about 6 million people scattered all over speak it. If someone should say "Saluton!" to you, say it back. It means "Hello" in Esperanto!

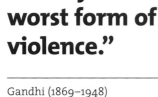

"Poverty is the worst form of violence."

Gandhi (1869–1948)

Today's World

Ulysse Mérou is a member of the first expedition beyond our solar system. The young journalist and his team land on Soror, a planet that looks like Earth, where they discover human beings who are very primitive—they live without any clothes and they can't talk. Then Ulysse and the other members of the expedition are captured by gorillas and brought to a city. There they find cars, planes, cameras, all belonging to the apes, who have reached a high degree of development. Ulysse realizes that on Soror the apes are the civilized ones and the humans have regressed bit by bit into animals. That's the beginning of the novel *Planet of the Apes*, by Pierre Boulle. Is it science fiction? Or prophecy?

HOMO SAPIENS SAPIENS

There are nearly 7 billion people in the world today. Where do they live? What are their lives like? Why don't we all get along? There are so many things to know about the world we live in that will help you understand other people. We're all citizens of the world, no matter where we call home.

Whereas the peoples of the United Nations have in the Charter reaffirmed their faith in fundamental human rights, in the dignity and worth of the human person and in the equal rights of men and women, and have determined to promote social progress and better standards of life in larger freedom…"

From *The Universal Declaration of Human Rights*, adopted by the United Nations on December 10, 1948.

Arctic Ocean

A World Full of People!

There have never been as many people in the world as there are now—6.6 billion!

People have not settled on the planet in a uniform way.
In order to grow things, they have preferred to live in temperate climates, on plains, by the sea, or along the banks of rivers. They have tried to avoid the deserts, high altitudes, or regions that are too hot or too cold. And yet there still are people everywhere!

NORTH AMERICA

New York

Mexico City

São Paulo

SOUTH AMERIC

An average **Colombian woman** will have two or three children. She can expect to live to age 75.

An average **Canadian woman** will have one or two children. She can expect to live to 84.

There are four times as many people in the world now as there were a hundred years ago. And the world's population keeps on growing! Every second of the day, there are three more humans on the planet. Populations grow fastest in the poorest countries of Asia and Africa. Women in these countries have more children than women in the rich countries of Europe and North America. They also have fewer resources to feed, educate, and keep their children healthy.

Today, one person out of six in the world lives in **India.**

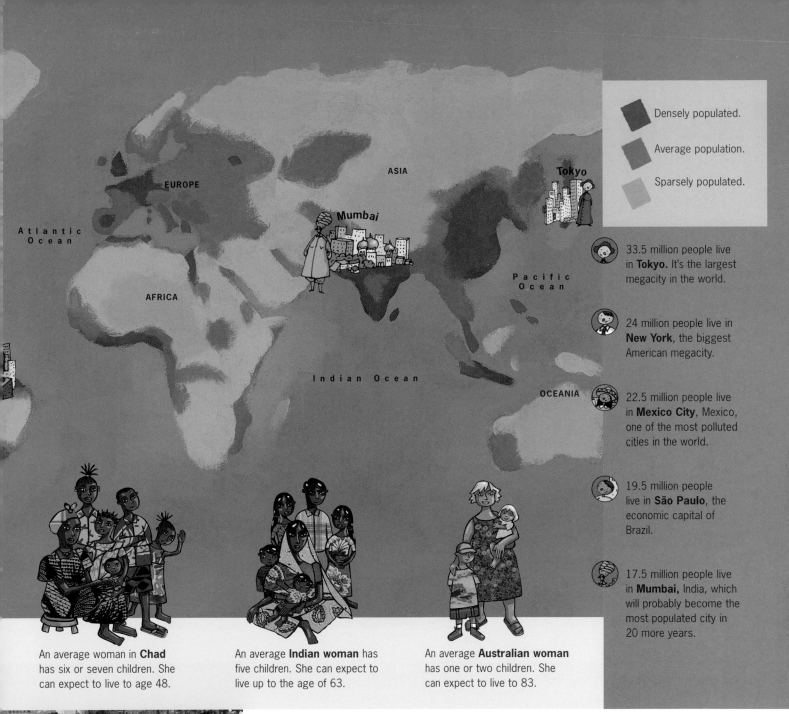

Densely populated.

Average population.

Sparsely populated.

EUROPE

ASIA

Tokyo

Mumbai

Atlantic
Ocean

AFRICA

Pacific
Ocean

Indian Ocean

OCEANIA

33.5 million people live in **Tokyo.** It's the largest megacity in the world.

24 million people live in **New York**, the biggest American megacity.

22.5 million people live in **Mexico City**, Mexico, one of the most polluted cities in the world.

19.5 million people live in **São Paulo**, the economic capital of Brazil.

17.5 million people live in **Mumbai**, India, which will probably become the most populated city in 20 more years.

An average woman in **Chad** has six or seven children. She can expect to live to age 48.

An average **Indian woman** has five children. She can expect to live up to the age of 63.

An average **Australian woman** has one or two children. She can expect to live to 83.

Everywhere, people leave the countryside to live in the city. They are seeking a better life and a chance to earn more money—though that is not always the way that it works out. Today, one person out of two on our planet lives in a city, and there are 435 cities across the globe with more than 1 million inhabitants. Some of these cities—like Tokyo (Japan) or São Paulo (Brazil)—are spread out in all directions, with never-ending suburbs. Continually spreading cities with 10 million to over 20 million inhabitants are called "megacities."

Europe

Europe is not a true continent but the western part of the enormous continent of Eurasia. In the east, the Ural Mountains separate Europe from Asia.

Area: 10,400,000 km² (4,015,754 miles²)

Population: 733 million

Largest Country: Russian Federation

Highest Mountain: Mount Elbrus, 5,642 m (18,510 ft.)

Longest River: Volga, 3,700 km (2,299 miles)

Europe does not have much oil, except in the North Sea. **Oil rig platforms** have been built to drill for this "black gold."

Four out of five Europeans live in cities. But traditional ways of life still exist, as in this **Portuguese fishing scene.**

The **Notting Hill Carnival, in London** (Great Britain), was created by immigrants from the Caribbean.

Europe has a mostly temperate climate, many rivers, fertile lands, and natural riches that keep people living there while attracting newcomers. Very few parts of Europe are uninhabited, except perhaps the far north, which is extremely cold. The rest is very densely populated.

Tundra
Prairie
Boreal Forest
Temperate Zone
Mediterranean Zone

The first factories were built in northwest Europe in the 19th century. Today, the **German automobile industry** is very important in the world market.

Atlantic Ocean

IRELAND
GREAT BRITAIN
PORTUGAL
SPAIN

FINLAND

RUSSIAN
FEDERATION

ESTONIA

NORWAY

SWEDEN

LATVIA

North Sea

DENMARK

LITHUANIA

Baltic Sea

KALININGRAD
RUSSIAN FEDERATION

BELARUS

HOLLAND

Rhine

POLAND

BELGIUM

GERMANY

LUXEMBOURG

UKRAINE

Dniper

Volga

CZECH
REPUBLIC

SLOVAKIA

FRANCE

SWITZERLAND

AUSTRIA

MOLDAVIA

Mont
Blanc

SLOVENIA

HUNGARY

ROMANIA

Black Sea

CROATIA

Danube

Mont
Elbrouz

BOSNIA-
HERZEGOVINA

SERBIA

BULGARIA

ITALY

MONTENEGRO

MACEDONIA

ALBANIA

Mediterranean Sea

GREECE

○ Stonehenge

○ Big Ben and Westminster
Palace, London

○ Chateau de Chambord

○ Alhambra Palace,
Grenada

○ Roman Coliseum

○ Mt. Etna volcano, Sicily

○ The Parthenon, Athens

○ St. Basil's Basilica,
Moscow

The Ukraine is called "the breadbasket of
Europe." Even though production is down,
wheat is still the symbol of food in Europe.

Whether it's to Paris,
London, or the city
of **Venice**, tourists
flock to Europe's
famous destinations.

Europeans today mostly
live in cities and few of them still
work the land. The large, rich cities
of western Europe—like
London, Paris, and Berlin—attract
immigrant workers from the
south, east, and other continents.
The borders between countries are
easily crossed and, recently, they
have changed dramatically: 13 new
countries have been created in
eastern Europe since 1990.

The European Union

The flag of the European Union was designed in 1986. Twelve stars in a circle represent the member nations.

The European Union (EU) is made up of 27 countries with a population of 490 million inhabitants. Its economic power rivals that of the United States.

The 27 member states of the European Union and their date of entry:

BELGIUM 1957
10.4 million inhabitants
Capital: Brussels
Principal languages: Flemish, French
Size: 30,500 km²
(11,777 miles²)
MONEY

FRANCE 1957
63 million inhabitants
Capital: Paris
Principal language French
Size: 551,500 km²
(212,951 miles²)
MONEY

GERMANY 1957
82.4 million inhabitants
Capital: Berlin
Principal language: German
Size: 357,030 km²
(137,860 miles²)
MONEY

ITALY 1957
58.1 million inhabitants
Capital: Rome
Principal language: Italian
Size: 301,340 km²
(116,356 miles²)
MONEY

In **1957,** twelve years after the end of the Second World War, six European countries got together to form the European Economic Community (EEC). Their goal was to keep the peace and permit easier trade among themselves. Today, merchandise flows freely in the member states, without being taxed at the borders. The citizens of the European Union (the name was changed in 1992), are also free to go where they wish, and even live and work in whichever country they wish.

Since January 2002, **the euro is the money that is used in the "euro zone":** Austria, Belgium, Finland, France, Germany, Greece, Ireland, Italy, Luxembourg, The Netherlands, Portugal, Slovenia, Spain.

LUXEMBOURG 1957
475,000 inhabitants
Capital: Luxembourg
Principal languages: French, Luxembourgeois
Size: 2,586 km²
(998 miles²)
MONEY

DENMARK 1973
5.4 million inhabitants
Capital: Copenhagen
Principal language: Danish
Danish crown
Size: 43,090 km²
(16,638 miles²)
MONEY

GREAT BRITAIN 1973
59.9 million inhabitants
Capital: London
Principal language English
Pound sterling
Size: 242,910 km²
(93,795 miles²)
MONEY

PORTUGAL 1986
10.6 million inhabitants
Capital: Lisbon
Principal language: Portuguese
Size: 91,980 km²
(35,516 miles²)
MONEY

THE NETHERLANDS 1957
16.3 million inhabitants
Capital: Amsterdam
Principal language: Dutch
Size: 41,530 km²
(16,036 miles²)
MONEY

IRELAND 1973
4 million inhabitants
Capital: Dublin
Principal language: English
Size: 70,270 km²
(27,133 miles²)
MONEY

GREECE 1981
11 million inhabitants
Capital: Athens
Principal language: Modern Greek
Size: 131,960 km²
(50,954 miles²)
MONEY

SPAIN 1986
43.2 million inhabitants
Capital: Madrid
Principal language: Spain
Size: 505,990 km²
(195,378 miles²)
MONEY

With the exception of the United Kingdom and Ireland, all of the countries that became members of the European Union before 2004 are part of the **Schengen agreement. In these countries, there are no more border crossings** and their citizens can travel freely from one country to the other. In addition, the Schengen countries cooperate to provide better security in all of their territories.

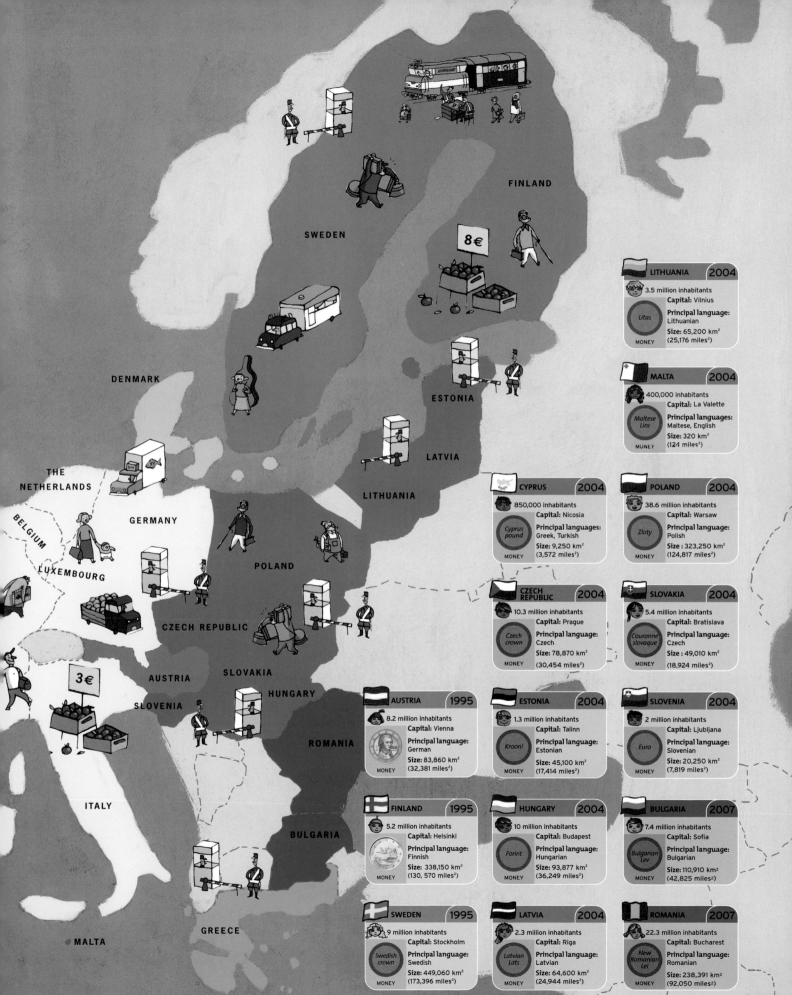

THE NETHERLANDS

BELGIUM

LUXEMBOURG

GERMANY

DENMARK

SWEDEN

FINLAND

8€

ESTONIA

LATVIA

LITHUANIA

POLAND

CZECH REPUBLIC

AUSTRIA

SLOVAKIA

SLOVENIA

HUNGARY

ROMANIA

ITALY

BULGARIA

3€

MALTA

GREECE

CYPRUS

LITHUANIA 2004
3.5 million inhabitants
Capital: Vilnius
Principal language: Lithuanian
Size: 65,200 km²
(25,176 miles²)
Litas MONEY

MALTA 2004
400,000 inhabitants
Capital: La Valette
Principal languages: Maltese, English
Size: 320 km²
(124 miles²)
Maltese Lira MONEY

CYPRUS 2004
850,000 inhabitants
Capital: Nicosia
Principal languages: Greek, Turkish
Size: 9,250 km²
(3,572 miles²)
Cyprus pound MONEY

POLAND 2004
38.6 million inhabitants
Capital: Warsaw
Principal language: Polish
Size: 323,250 km²
(124,817 miles²)
Zloty MONEY

CZECH REPUBLIC 2004
10.3 million inhabitants
Capital: Prague
Principal language: Czech
Size: 78,870 km²
(30,454 miles²)
Czech crown MONEY

SLOVAKIA 2004
5.4 million inhabitants
Capital: Bratislava
Principal language: Czech
Size: 49,010 km²
(18,924 miles²)
Couronne slovaque MONEY

AUSTRIA 1995
8.2 million inhabitants
Capital: Vienna
Principal language: German
Size: 83,860 km²
(32,381 miles²)
MONEY

ESTONIA 2004
1.3 million inhabitants
Capital: Talinn
Principal language: Estonian
Size: 45,100 km²
(17,414 miles²)
Krooni MONEY

SLOVENIA 2004
2 million inhabitants
Capital: Ljubljana
Principal language: Slovenian
Size: 20,250 km²
(7,819 miles²)
Euro MONEY

FINLAND 1995
5.2 million inhabitants
Capital: Helsinki
Principal language: Finnish
Size: 338,150 km²
(130, 570 miles²)
MONEY

HUNGARY 2004
10 million inhabitants
Capital: Budapest
Principal language: Hungarian
Size: 93,877 km²
(36,249 miles²)
Forint MONEY

BULGARIA 2007
7.4 million inhabitants
Capital: Sofia
Principal language: Bulgarian
Size: 110,910 km²
(42,825 miles²)
Bulgarian lev MONEY

SWEDEN 1995
9 million inhabitants
Capital: Stockholm
Principal language: Swedish
Size: 449,060 km²
(173,396 miles²)
Swedish crown MONEY

LATVIA 2004
2.3 million inhabitants
Capital: Riga
Principal language: Latvian
Size: 64,600 km²
(24,944 miles²)
Latvian Lats MONEY

ROMANIA 2007
22.3 million inhabitants
Capital: Bucharest
Principal language: Romanian
Size: 238,391 km²
(92,050 miles²)
New Romanian Lei MONEY

Africa

The population of Africa is growing faster than anywhere else. There are many more young Africans than old ones. Feeding and taking care of everyone is not always easy.

Size: 30 million km² (12 million miles²)

Population: 915 million

Largest Country: Sudan

Highest Mountain: Kilimanjaro, 5,895 m (19,340 ft.)

Longest River: The Nile, also the longest river in the world. 6,695 km (4,184 miles).

This warm continent is covered in many parts by desert where water resources are scarce. It is certainly more difficult to live here and grow food than it is in a temperate climate. But not all of Africa is completely dry. Around the equator, there are areas that are fertile and green, and there are fields and forests kept moist by strong and frequent rains.

With an area of more than 8 million km² (3,089,042 miles²), the **Sahara** is by far the biggest desert in the world. And it continues to spread.

MOROCCO

ALGERIA

MAURITANIA

MALI

SENEGAL

GAMBIA

GUINEA-BISSAU

GUINEA

Niger

BURKINA FASO

SIERRA LEON

LIBERIA

IVORY COAST

GHANA

TOGO

BENIN

Atlantic Ocean

○ Casablanca Mosque

○ Tassili rock painting

○ Dogon cliff-dwellers at Bandiagara

○ Yamoussoukro Basilica

● Pyramids and Sphinx at Giza

○ Suez Canal

○ Victoria Falls

In the city of **Abidjan (Ivory Coast)**, traditional clothing and practices mix with skyscrapers.

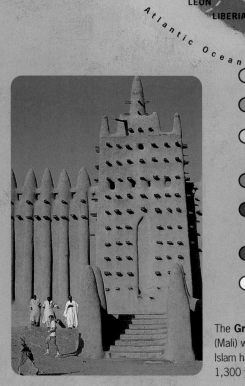

The **Great Mosque of Djenné** (Mali) was built in the 13th century. Islam has been practiced in Africa for 1,300 years and continues to grow.

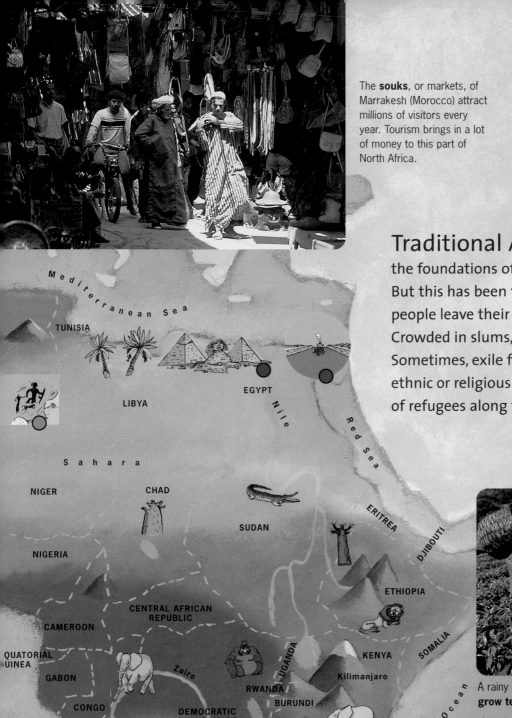

The **souks**, or markets, of Marrakesh (Morocco) attract millions of visitors every year. Tourism brings in a lot of money to this part of North Africa.

	Desert
	Savanna
	Tropical Forest
	Mediterranean Zone

Traditional African life is built on the foundations of tribe, dialect, and village. But this has been turned upside down as more people leave their villages and settle in the cities. Crowded in slums, they rarely find a better life. Sometimes, exile from home is even sadder: ethnic or religious conflicts create long lines of refugees along the roads.

Mediterranean Sea

TUNISIA

LIBYA

EGYPT

Nile

Red Sea

Sahara

NIGER

CHAD

SUDAN

ERITREA

DJIBOUTI

NIGERIA

ETHIOPIA

CENTRAL AFRICAN REPUBLIC

CAMEROON

SOMALIA

QUATORIAL UINEA

UGANDA

KENYA

Zaire

GABON

RWANDA

Kilimanjaro

CONGO

BURUNDI

DEMOCRATIC REPUBLIC OF CONGO

Indian Ocean

TANZANIA

ZAMBIA

ANGOLA

MALAWI

Zambezi

NAMIBIA

ZIMBABWE

MADAGASCAR

BOTSWANA

MOZAMBIQUE

SWAZILAND

LESOTHO

SOUTH AFRICA

A rainy climate in Kenya makes it possible to **grow tea**. This harvest will be sold overseas.

These two women in Mali **crush millet** in a village scene that is typical of traditional Africa.

157

Salif Lives in Mali

Salif Koulibaly is eleven years old. He lives in Semafala, a village near the town of Segou, 240 km (149 miles) away from the capital, Bamako.

Salif's family lives in houses of adobe (a mix of clay, rocks, and straw). There are eleven people in the family: Salif, his father, his mother, and his five brothers and sisters, as well as his father's second wife and her two children.

The majority of Malians are Muslims. Their religion allows men to have more than one wife. They are "polygamous."

Salif wakes up very early, at 5:30 a.m., because it takes him more than an hour to get to school. For breakfast, he has a mango with his brothers and sisters. His dad, who is a nurse, has already left on a scooter to visit nearby villages.

Only one in four Mali villagers are vaccinated against dangerous diseases. Yellow fever still causes a great many deaths.

At school the students wear a uniform. Today, Salif only has a morning class. His teacher will take another class in the afternoon.

One out of every two Malians is under the age of 15. That is a lot of students! There aren't enough schools and teachers to take care of all of them at the same time.

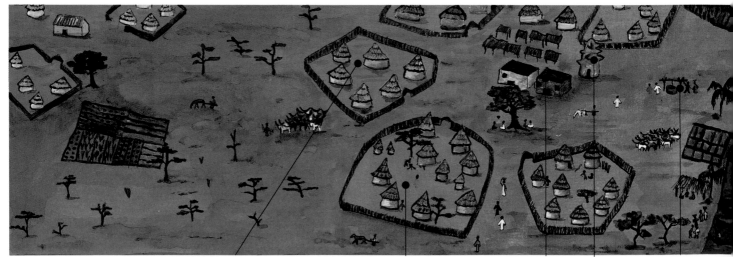

Salif's household   **Chief of Semafala's household**   **Health center**   **Mosque**   **Wells**

Salif and his father cross the Niger River in a dugout to visit his uncle's village. For dinner they'll have "saame," a dish of rice and fish.

Most dishes are based on grains (millet, wheat, sorghum, or rice) accompanied by various sauces made of shea butter or baobab leaves.

After lunch (a meal of rice with a peanut-based sauce), Salif plays with his "flan bolo," a group of friends his own age.

With no new toys available, young Malians make do with whatever they find: cans, boxes, and plastic corks, among other things.

A **motorcycle** made of tin cans and bicycle chains.

Salif comes back to his home where he finds his sisters. They didn't go to school because they had to do chores and fetch water.

Drinking water is very precious. During the dry season, the wells are empty and it's necessary to walk very far to find any.

After dinner, everyone gets together to listen to the griot tell the story of Da Monzon, an ancient warrior chief.

Griots are storytellers, singers, and musicians who pass the history of the tribe from generation to generation. They are the "memory" of Africa.

The **kora** is a griot's instrument, a cross between a harp and a lute, with 21 strings.

The Niger River   **Salif's uncle's village**

Asia and the Middle East

From the frozen tundra of Siberia to the tropical jungles of the Southeast, from the greatest wealth to the most abject poverty, from Islam to Buddhism—Asia is a continent of infinite diversity.

Area: 44,000,000 km² (16,989,728 miles²)

Population: 4 billion

Largest Country: Russian Federation (Asian part)

Highest Mountain: Mount Everest, 8,850 m (29,035 ft.), the tallest mountain in the world.

Longest River: Chang Jiang 6,211 km (3859 miles)

Buddhism was founded in India in the 6th century B.C.E. **Buddhist monks** wear saffron robes.

In Saudi Arabia, money earned from oil is used to expand agriculture despite the climatic conditions. This is the world's biggest cow farm.

Mediterranean Sea
Black Sea
TURKEY
CYPRUS
GEORGIA
ARMENIA AZERBAIJAN
Caspian Sea
KAZAKHSTAN
LEBANON SYRIA
ISRAEL
JORDAN
IRAQ
IRAN
UZBEKISTAN
TURKMENISTAN
KIRGHIZSTAN
TADJIKISTAN
AFGHANISTAN
KUWAIT
BAHRAIN
QATAR
UNITED ARAB EMIRATES
Red Sea
SAUDIA ARABIA
Sea of Oman
PAKISTAN
Evere
NEPAL
Ganges
OMAN
Indian Ocean
YEMEN
INDIA
SRI LANKA
MALDIVES
Ob

Asia and the Middle East make the largest and most populated of the continents. Sixty-two times the size of the state of Texas, one out of five of the world's inhabitants lives in this region, especially in India and China—the only two countries who have populations of more than 1 billion each. Yet there are also areas that are practically deserted, like Siberia, the steppes of central Asia, the Arabian plateau, and the Himalayan Mountains.

India's high tech workers are very advanced. They are often recruited by Western companies, especially by Americans.

160

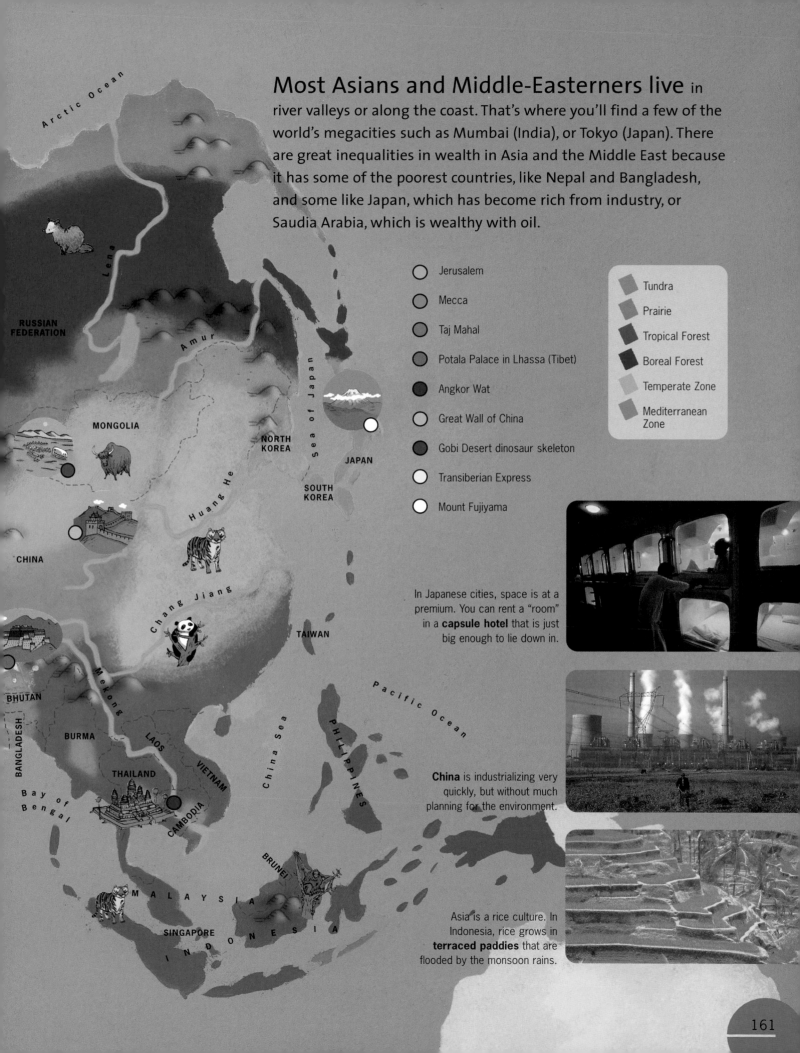

Most Asians and Middle-Easterners live in river valleys or along the coast. That's where you'll find a few of the world's megacities such as Mumbai (India), or Tokyo (Japan). There are great inequalities in wealth in Asia and the Middle East because it has some of the poorest countries, like Nepal and Bangladesh, and some like Japan, which has become rich from industry, or Saudia Arabia, which is wealthy with oil.

○ Jerusalem

○ Mecca

○ Taj Mahal

○ Potala Palace in Lhassa (Tibet)

● Angkor Wat

○ Great Wall of China

● Gobi Desert dinosaur skeleton

○ Transiberian Express

○ Mount Fujiyama

Tundra

Prairie

Tropical Forest

Boreal Forest

Temperate Zone

Mediterranean Zone

Arctic Ocean

Lena

RUSSIAN FEDERATION

Amur

MONGOLIA

Sea of Japan

NORTH KOREA

JAPAN

SOUTH KOREA

Huang He

CHINA

Chang Jiang

TAIWAN

Pacific Ocean

Mekong

BHUTAN

BANGLADESH

BURMA

LAOS

VIETNAM

THAILAND

China Sea

PHILIPPINES

Bay of Bengal

CAMBODIA

BRUNEI

MALAYSIA

SINGAPORE

INDONESIA

In Japanese cities, space is at a premium. You can rent a "room" in a **capsule hotel** that is just big enough to lie down in.

China is industrializing very quickly, but without much planning for the environment.

Asia is a rice culture. In Indonesia, rice grows in **terraced paddies** that are flooded by the monsoon rains.

161

Parichat lives in Thailand

Parichat Prathet is ten years old. Along with her parents and her little brother, she lives in Bangkok, the capital of Thailand. They live in a house on stilts on the banks of the Chao Phraya River.

Parichat gets up early. She needs lots of time to get to school: 15 minutes on the river bus, and another hour on a city bus in heavy traffic.

With six million people and very old cars, Bangkok is crowded and polluted.

Finally, at school! Before going into class, Parichat and her friends listen to the national anthem and salute the flag to show their loyalty to the Royal Family.

King Bhumibol Adulyadej has reigned over Thailand since the 1950s. His portrait hangs in all stores.

Morning classes begin: Thai reading and writing, English, and arithmetic.

Thai parents often have a hard time paying for school uniforms and books. Yet nine out of ten children go to school.

River bus

City bus

It's lunch time. There's no cafeteria so Parichat finds a food vendor and buys some sticky rice, some chicken kebabs, and a bag of sliced pineapple.

Food isn't very expensive in Thailand. The lunch that Parichat has bought cost 40 bahts, or about $1.25.

When she gets home, Parichat helps her mother decorate the "house of spirits.

In the front of many Thai homes, there's a little house of spirits that looks like a temple. The spirit, or "phi" of the home lives here. The spirit house is often honored with flowers and decorations.

The **Krathong** is a boat in the shape of a lotus flower on which people put candles, incense and a coin.

Parichat adores school in the afternoon. After a class of Thai dance, she and the other students build little boats to carry lights on the Chao Phraya for the feast of Loy Krathong.

Loy Krathong is a festival of water and light at the end of the rainy season. It takes place on the full Moon in the month of November.

In the evening, Parichat and her parents have dinner at a restaurant run by friends. They'll have curried pork, chicken with cashew nuts, shrimp marinated in coconut milk, and fried rice. Each item is served in plates on the table.

Thai cooking is famous all over the world. Some people might find it too spicy. The tiny "phrik khi nu" pepper is fiercely hot!

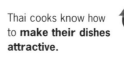

Thai cooks know how to **make their dishes attractive.**

Parichat's school　　　　**food vendor**

North and South America

Forest and virgin lands cover more than three-quarters of Canada, the second largest country in the world.

Area: 40,000,000 km² (15,445,208 miles²)

Population: 900 million

Largest Country: Canada

Highest Mountain: Aconcagua, 6,962 m (22,841 ft.)

Longest River: Amazon 7,000 km (4,350 miles)

The two American continents run from the North Pole to the South Pole. In between are a vast range of different climates and landscapes.

The main language of North America is English. In Canada, French is spoken in Quebec and is the second offical language of the country. In Central and South America, people speak mostly Spanish, except in Brazil, where they speak Portuguese. These differences in language reflect the different colonizers who came to the continents from Europe. Nowadays, the New World is made up of the descendants of those colonizers and the slaves who were brought over from Africa, the Native people who were there before the Europeans arrived, and immigrants from every nation of the world.

From the **barriadas** of Lima (Peru), to the **favellas** of São Paulo (Brazil), the large cities of South America are surrounded by slums where the poor live.

In the Atacama desert in Chile—one of the driest on the planet— you'll find the **Chuquicamata mine,** the largest copper mine in the world.

On the **plains of the Pampas in Argentina,** huge flocks of sheep are watched over by gauchos, Argentina's cowboys.

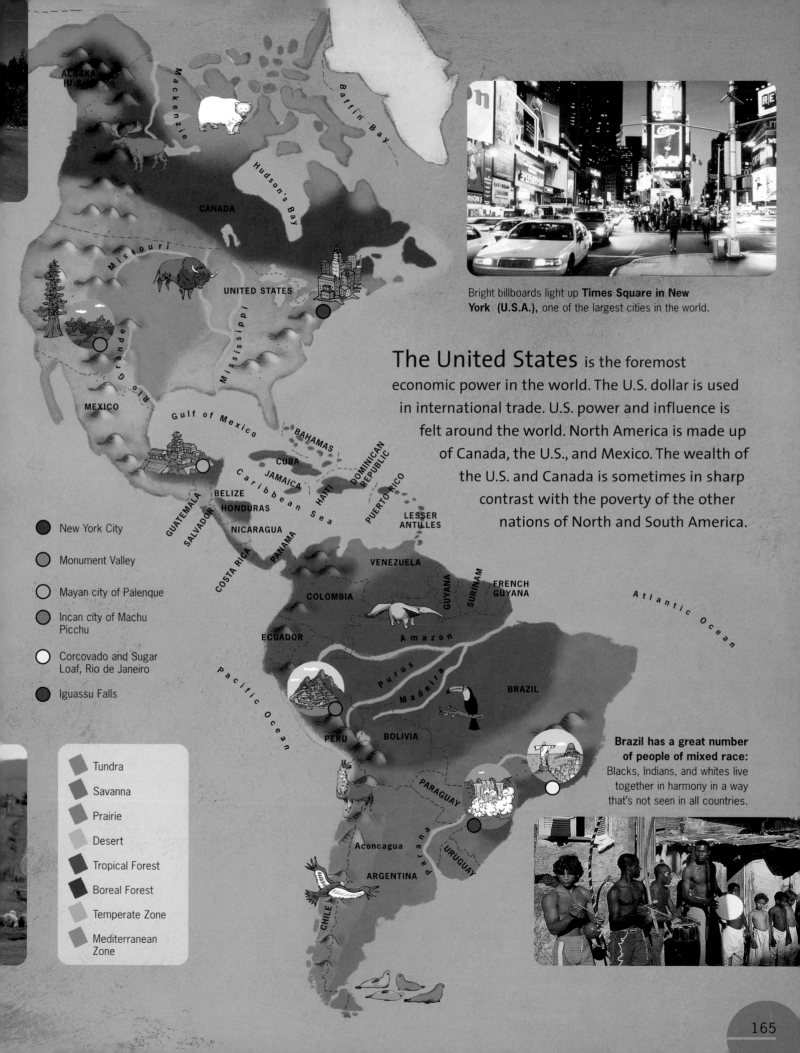

Bright billboards light up **Times Square in New York (U.S.A.),** one of the largest cities in the world.

The United States is the foremost economic power in the world. The U.S. dollar is used in international trade. U.S. power and influence is felt around the world. North America is made up of Canada, the U.S., and Mexico. The wealth of the U.S. and Canada is sometimes in sharp contrast with the poverty of the other nations of North and South America.

ALASKA (U.S.A.)

Mackenzie

Baffin Bay

Hudson's Bay

CANADA

Missouri

UNITED STATES

Mississippi

Rio Grande

MEXICO

Gulf of Mexico

BAHAMAS

CUBA

JAMAICA

DOMINICAN REPUBLIC

HAITI

PUERTO RICO

Caribbean Sea

BELIZE

GUATEMALA

HONDURAS

SALVADOR

NICARAGUA

COSTA RICA

PANAMA

LESSER ANTILLES

VENEZUELA

COLOMBIA

GUYANA

SURINAM

FRENCH GUYANA

Atlantic Ocean

ECUADOR

Amazon

Purus

Madeira

BRAZIL

Pacific Ocean

PERU

BOLIVIA

PARAGUAY

Parana

Aconcagua

ARGENTINA

URUGUAY

CHILE

- ● New York City
- ● Monument Valley
- ○ Mayan city of Palenque
- ● Incan city of Machu Picchu
- ○ Corcovado and Sugar Loaf, Rio de Janeiro
- ● Iguassu Falls

Tundra

Savanna

Prairie

Desert

Tropical Forest

Boreal Forest

Temperate Zone

Mediterranean Zone

Brazil has a great number of people of mixed race: Blacks, Indians, and whites live together in harmony in a way that's not seen in all countries.

KNOW-IT-ALL NEWS

Vera Smart
Editor-in-chief

Ashley Asks
Interviewer

Tex A. Snap
Photo Journalist

Claire Itty
Researcher

Art Phul
Illustrator

Ed Shorter
News Briefs

From the Editor's Desk

Every country in the world that calls itself a democracy holds elections to choose its leaders. All its citizens have the right to vote for the people they want in government. They run the country and oversee things like education, health care, and defense.

Vera Smart

Let's Go to the Polls!

Max goes to vote on Election Day

Max is 22 years old. He believes it's important to exercise his right to vote and makes sure he doesn't miss an election day.

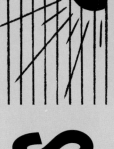

Art Phul

He hasn't made up his mind about who to vote for, so on his way to the polling station at the local school, he reads the election posters that have been put up by each candidate.

The Scoop

33.3 % voted for John Colby.

Who didn't vote for me???

Terms of Office

Americans vote for President every four years. Canada, England, Australia, and other countries have a parliamentary system—so the leader of the party that wins the majority becomes Prime Minister. A parliamentary government must call an election at least once in five years.

Ed Shorter

Voting Words

Democracy
A government of officials chosen by the people through the election process.

Candidate
A person running for elected office.

Ballot
A list of candidates to choose from in the voting booth.

Political Party
An organization of people with similar political beliefs who band together to try to get elected.

Voter

A citizen of a country, of the legal age in that country to cast a ballot, who exercises his or her right to vote.

When he enters, Max presents his i.d. and his name is checked against a list of registered voters. He had to register his intention to vote in his locality long before the election.

Alone in the polling booth, Max reads his ballot and thinks about the candidates before marking his choice.

Max takes his folded up ballot over to the polling box and puts it into the slot. His vote is secret and he doesn't have to tell anyone who he voted for.

After the polls close, he goes to watch the results on TV with some friends. The candidate Max didn't vote for gets 50.4% of the vote, or more than half of all the votes cast, and is elected. Max is disappointed that his party didn't win—it was so close!

Tex A. Snap

News Briefs

Voter turnout Not everyone casts his or her ballot on election day. In the United States, 50% of eligible voters showing up at the polls is considered a good turnout. In Canada, that number is more than 60%. In Australia, it is against the law to not vote, so turnout is 95%.

Who can vote? In most countries, you must be at least 18 years old to vote. Women can vote everywhere in the world, but they couldn't until 1918 in Canada and Great Britain, and until 1920 in the U.S. New Zealand was the first country to give women the vote, in 1893.

Citizenship You have to be a citizen of a country to vote in its elections, which means either being born there or having lived there for a certain number of years. Voting is one of the privileges of citizenship.

Ed Shorter

Ashley Asks

Margaret Chow, an election official.

How is the way a person votes changing?
Paper ballots, punch cards, and lever pulls are disappearing. They're being replaced in polling booths by touch screen machines and optical scanners. It's the beginning of e-voting.

Do you mean I'll be able to vote on the Internet?
No. You'll still have to go to a polling station so we can be sure you are who you say you are. You'll still cast your vote behind a screen or curtain to assure your privacy. And your vote won't be posted on the World Wide Web—it'll just be counted on that machine and sent to election headquarters.

Can anyone change my vote?
There have been a lot of fears that e-voting machines aren't tamper proof, and that a clever hacker can program one to count votes differently than they are cast. But that has never happened and election officials are working to make sure it never does. Most e-voting machines print out a paper ballot as a back-up receipt.

José Lives in Mexico City

> José Arraya is twelve years old. He lives with his parents, his three sisters, and his grandmother in Mexico City. The city and its surrounding area is home to 23 million people.

José's mother wakes him up for school on weekdays. Their family is quite typical—the average household in Mexico City is between 7 and 10 people.

Most Mexicans are descendants of the Aztecs who first lived in the area, and the Spanish, who colonized the country beginning in the 16th century.

José's favorite subject at school is natural science. And he learns math, history, and Spanish grammar and literature.

Mexican schools also emphasize sports, with soccer, basketball, and track events several times a week.

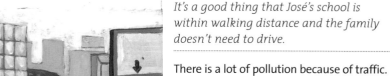

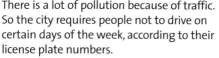

It's a good thing that José's school is within walking distance and the family doesn't need to drive.

There is a lot of pollution because of traffic. So the city requires people not to drive on certain days of the week, according to their license plate numbers.

It's lunch time. José brings a chicken burrito from home, but he can't resist an order of fries.

A burrito is a wheat or corn tortilla (a flatbread cooked on a griddle) that is rolled up around meat or beans.

Mexicans love **hot spices**. How about a snack of pineapple spiced with chilies?

After school, José relaxes by watching sports on TV. He'll finish his homework and then he'll go outside to play soccer with his friends.

There are five professional soccer teams in the city. It's also popular with Mexicans to go to the bullfights and the rodeo.

There's a party at the Arrayas tonight. José's oldest sister is turning 15, so she's having her quinceañera celebrations. The family will go to mass together and then come home for tamales and cake.

Mexico is a very Catholic country. People celebrate family events and holidays by going to church.

When it gets dark, José's mother calls for him to say goodbye to his friends and come indoors.

Like many big cities, Mexico City has its share of crime. Families look out for their kids and make sure they are safe.

school

Oceania

Oceania is made up of more than 20,000 islands. Some are mountainous and volcanic. Others are coral reefs.

Size: 9,000,000 km² (3,475,172 miles²)

Population: 33.3 million

Largest Country: Australia

Highest Mountain: Mount Wilhelm 4,509 m (14,793 ft.), Papua New Guinea

Longest River: Murray 2,575 km (1,600 miles)

Australia is the largest island in Oceania—and the largest island in the world. Next to Australia are two other large, mountainous islands: Papua New Guinea and New Zealand. The thousands of other little islands that make up Oceania are scattered throughout the Pacific, between Asia and the Americas, most of them in the southern hemisphere. There are three main groups: Melanesia, Micronesia, and Polynesia. Some are independent, others belong to foreign powers. Some serve as military bases.

■ Savanna

■ Prairie

■ Tropical Forest

■ Mediterranean Zone

PALAU

Mt. Wilhelm

○ Sydney Opera House

● Ayers Rock, or Uluru

○ Rotorua Geysers

Australia is **three-quarters desert.** Enormous trucks with multiple trailers carry merchandise and cattle across long distances. There is a wealth of natural resources such as coal, iron, bauxite, and uranium here.

AUSTRALIA

Darling

Murray

Indian Ocean

Aborigines are the oldest inhabitants of Australia. English colonizers who arrived in the 18th century chased them bit by bit off their lands. There are few Aborigines left, and many live in extreme poverty.

The 3.3 million inhabitants of the many small Pacific islands live mostly off fishing and farming sugar cane, bananas, and coconuts. The beautiful landscapes of Polynesia also attract many tourists. But all of their wealth combined pales by comparison to Australia, the giant island of 7,700,000 km² (2.973,202 miles²). Australia's population of 20 million lives mostly in cities in the southwest and along the coasts. The world's largest flock of sheep lives here, and grain farming is ultra-modern.

Even though the French and the English ran the government of the **Vanuatu** islands until 1980, **village life has stayed traditional.** Villagers are led by a chief and stick close together. Children are protected by their parents and by the whole community.

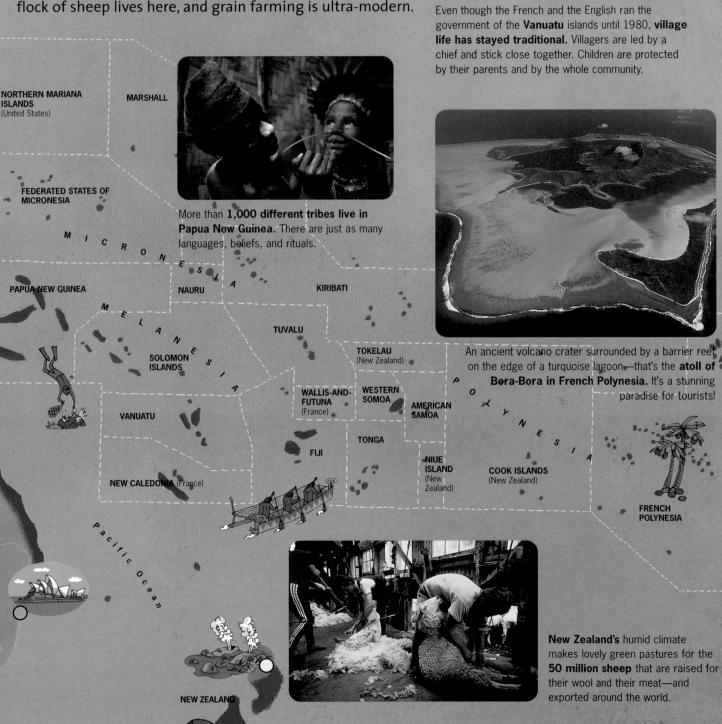

More than **1,000 different tribes live in Papua New Guinea.** There are just as many languages, beliefs, and rituals.

An ancient volcano crater surrounded by a barrier reef on the edge of a turquoise lagoon—that's the **atoll of Bora-Bora in French Polynesia.** It's a stunning paradise for tourists!

New Zealand's humid climate makes lovely green pastures for the **50 million sheep** that are raised for their wool and their meat—and exported around the world.

171

The World at War

Thousands of people are hurt or killed in wars every year. Men, women, and children are forced to leave their homes and become refugees.

Why do wars happen ?

War keeps farmers and business people from doing their jobs. **Food becomes scarce**, and refugees rely on it being brought in from abroad.

In one country, there may be two groups fighting against each other in a **civil war** for control of resources and political power. That's the situation in Angola.

Sometimes **two ethnic groups don't get along and confront each other.** This can lead to genocide, or the massacre of one part of the population by another. This is what happened in Rwanda in 1994–1995.

Here, long **lines of civilians** walk along the roadways. As a result of war, 21 million people in the world are displaced today.

War destroys homes. In camps, refugees, who have lost everything, live in plastic tents.

International humanitarian organizations set up camps for refugees. Their safety is assured by the **blue helmets** of the United Nations.

Twenty-first century weapons are murderous. Atomic and chemical weapons pose a threat to all of humanity. Their danger may be keeping leaders from launching all-out world war. On the other hand, there are dozens of "little" wars raging throughout the world. Many small countries are torn by civil war.

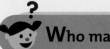

Who makes weapons ?

The biggest arms dealers in the world are the United States, Russia, France, Germany, and the United Kingdom. In 2005, weapons sales were worth over $40 billion. Prices ranged from $6.50 for a grenade, to $2.5 billion for an aircraft carrier. The biggest buyers are countries that are at peace and want to protect themselves, such as Saudi Arabia, Taiwan, the People's Republic of China, Greece, and Turkey. Poor countries that are at war may resort to illegal weapons dealers to arm themselves.

One part of the country wishes to separate from the rest. The inhabitants launch a **war of independence**. That's what's happening between Chechnya and the Russian Federation.

Two or more governments may fight to **conquer or regain lost territory.** India and Pakistan have been in that kind of war over the state of Kashmir.

Sometimes a conflict has **many causes**: religious disagreements, conquest of a territory, a fight about power. That's the case in the Middle East between the Israelis and the Palestinians.

War separates families. People put up photos of their **missing** loved ones, hoping for news.

Because of war, more than 1 million children became **orphans** in the 20th century.

Doctors look after the **wounded**. Lack of hygiene and food may cause diseases such as cholera, plague, and dysentery.

173

Human Rights

Amnesty International, created in 1961, defends the rights of people in the world. The organization is opposed to torture and the death penalty.

Reporters Without Borders fights for journalists around the world to be able to do their work gathering news freely.

UNICEF, founded in 1946, tries to improve the lives of children in the poorer countries of the world.

In 1948, the United Nations adopted the Universal Declaration of Human Rights. It contains 30 articles that define the principal human rights across the world, including respect for the person, a right to life, and a right to liberty.

These rights are not respected everywhere, but they represent ideals that certain governments and groups try to uphold. In democratic countries like the United States or Canada, you can say whatever you want, children attend school, and people are paid for their work—though that doesn't mean that there's no poverty. In other countries, laws are much more repressive and the rights of citizens to live in dignity are not respected.

According to **Article 4** of the declaration, slavery is forbidden. Yet in Haiti, 100,000 children of poor villagers were sold to people in cities to work as unpaid servants.

SLAVERY IS FORBIDDEN

ALL BORN

That's **Article 1** of the declaration. But in India, society is divided into "castes," and some people are considered inferior to others.

Number Crunch

56 is the number of countries where a person can go to jail because of their opinions.

4,000 is how many people were sentenced to death in one recent year in China.

1.3 billion is the number of people in the world who live on less than $1 a day.

EVERYONE HAS THE RIGHT TO THINK AND SPEAK FREELY

This is **Article 19** of the declaration. But in Tunisia, there are journalists in jail because they questioned the government.

So says **Article 5** of the declaration. Yet, in 2001 in Russia, 10,000 prisoners died of malnutrition, illness, and mistreatement.

NOBODY SHOULD BE MISTREATED OR TORTURED

That's **Article 23** of the declaration. Yet in many countries, there are lots of people who don't have jobs.

This is what **Article 25** of the declaration states. But in some countries in Africa and Asia, people who have AIDS can't afford to pay for medicine.

EVERYONE SHOULD BE ABLE TO EARN ENOUGH TO HAVE A DECENT LIFE

EVERYONE HAS A RIGHT TO WORK

ALL CHILDREN HAVE A RIGHT TO FREE EDUCATION

PEOPLE ARE FREE AND HAVE EQUAL RIGHTS

That's according to **Article 26** of the declaration. But in Chad, only one in three girls attends school.

KNOW-IT-ALL NEWS

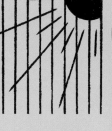

Vera Smart
Editor-in-chief

Ashley Asks
Interviewer

Tex A. Snap
Photo Journalist

Claire Itty
Researcher

Art Phul
Illustrator

Ed Shorter
News Briefs

From the Editor's Desk

"A child has a right to an education...and to be protected from all forms of exploitation," says the 1959 UN Declaration of the Rights of the Child. Yet today one child in five doesn't attend school, and 250 million children work.

Vera Smart

Art Phul

No More Child Labor!

Udayraj, 10 years old, factory worker

Udayraj doesn't go to school. He spends every day, from 4:00 in the morning to 10:00 at night working in a carpet factory in Kalakatar, India. The factory is guarded night and day to make sure no children escape.

A year ago, a recruiter came to Udayraj's village and spoke to his father. Udayraj's father couldn't feed his family because of a bad harvest.

So when the recruiter offered his father money for Udayraj and promised he would send the boy to school, Udayraj's father agreed.

Ashley Asks

Dinesh Krishna is with an organization opposed to child labor in South India.

Do a lot of children in India work?
We think there are about 130 million who do, and 50 million work in the most dangerous jobs. They earn less that $1 a day—when they're lucky enough to get paid.

What are you doing to stop it?
We have set up "children's villages," where children elect representatives to bargain with the adults who govern the actual village.

Child Soldiers

There are estimated to be 300,000 children fighting in armies, both boys and girls. They are recruited by force, sometimes from refugee camps.

Slavery

In Africa and Asia, some children are "given" to people to whom their parents owe money. It's called "indentured servitude," but it really is slavery.

Danger!

Most of the world's fireworks are made by children in two Chinese provinces: Hunan and Jiangxi. The children work almost 12 hours a day, exposed to toxic materials, not to mention the risk of explosion.

Ed Shorter

And what do these children's representatives ask for?

A ban on dangerous work, honoring the right to go to school, and better school environments, with more classes and books.

Do the adults listen?

Yes! But you must realize that Indian kids grow up much faster than North American ones. Indian girls can be married at 13!

The Scoop

A Children's Hero from Canada

At the age of 12, Craig Kielburger of Toronto heard about a boy in Pakistan his own age who was killed for speaking out against forcing kids to work. Craig organized 11 of his friends to campaign against child labor. The organization he founded in 1995, Free the Children, now has more than one million members in 45 countries helping children through education.

Ed Shorter

The work is hard and dangerous. There are a lot of woolen fibers in the factory and Udayraj has difficulty breathing. He also has to protect his eyes from the dyes—one drop and he'll go blind.

Udayraj can't even stop working to eat lunch. All he gets for lunch and dinner at the carpet factory is two pieces of flatbread and some salt. He'll be punished if he asks for more.

Tex A. Snap

Child Labor by the Numbers

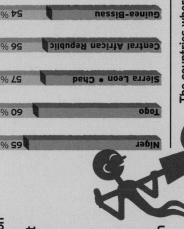

Country	%
Niger	65 %
Togo	60 %
Sierra Leon • Chad	57 %
Central African Republic	56 %
Guinea-Bissau	54 %
Cameroon	51 %
Ivory Coast	35 %
Uganda	34 %
Senegal	33 %
Somalia • Tanzania	32 %

The countries where the largest percentage of children between ages 5 and 14 are forced to work.

Child labor is common in some African and Asian countries. But that doesn't mean there isn't any in Europe or North America. There are child miners in Latin America, and child farm laborers in western American states like Arizona and California.

SuperSneaks
Best Deal in the World!
But do you know what the kids who made them had to go through?

$48

A Polluted Planet

Life in rich countries relies on factories and cars that pollute. And poor countries can't always afford to keep the environment clean.

A damaged oil freighter creates an **oil spill.** The ocean and coastlines are covered with oil, and fish and seabirds are killed.

In Africa, South America, and Asia, factories and farming companies **cut down forests** to use the wood and clear the land for agriculture.

People **throw away** plastic and glass, which take hundreds of years to decompose.

Until 1982, barrels of **nuclear waste** were tossed into the sea, creating danger of radiation underwater.

Every day we produce more and more and we consume more and more. Factories that make goods burn oil, gas, or coal and emit fumes into the air that are bad for our health and for the Earth's atmosphere. The sea is polluted by leaking oil and spills from oil tankers that are in bad shape. Farmers pollute the soil and rivers by using fertilizers and pesticides. Pollution is in the air, soil, water, and underground.

Smoke from power plants, factory chimneys, and traffic in the city pollutes the air.

Animal waste from farms in some countries flows underground, making **ground water undrinkable.**

Ecological movements have sounded the alarm. National leaders meet to find solutions to these problems by lowering gas emissions and finding less polluting sources of energy. But not everyone agrees. Some poor countries want to produce more and don't have the means to pollute less. Some rich countries are reluctant to make sacrifices to their comfortable way of life in order to bring about change.

Simple Ways to Respect the Earth:

Sort trash. Glass, paper, and cardboard can be recycled to make new things.

Don't take the car. Walk, ride your bike, or take public transit. Use **electricity** wisely to cut down pollution from power plants.

Use **natural fertilizers,** like compost, rather than chemical products.

Don't buy furniture made of exotic woods. Some tree species are disappearing.

Genius at Work!

They say that music tames the savage beast. Orpheus was an outstanding poet and musician. According to Greek legend, when he sang and played the lyre, his music was so lovely that all the animals followed him, the trees stopped swishing, and rivers stopped flowing. His song was even more enchanting than the one sung by the Sirens who stopped sailors on their course. And it was his music that calmed Cerebrus, the horrible three-headed dog that guards the gates of Hades, when Orpheus went there to find his wife, Eurydice. When he died, Zeus took his lyre and placed it in the heavens as the constellation Lyra. You can still see it shine at night.

Pygmalion, the legendary king of Cyprus, was also a famous sculptor. Disappointed in love, he decided to devote all his time to his art. But one day, he fell in love with one of his own works—a magnificent ivory statue of a young girl that had taken him a long time to sculpt and polish to perfection. He begged the goddess Aphrodite to bring the statue to life. The goddess agreed, and Pygmalion married Galatea. He had used his art to create a woman he never would have met.

The Cheops Pyramid at Giza in Egypt is the last of the Seven Wonders of the World. Maybe you've seen a picture of it next to the famous Sphinx. The six other wonders have been destroyed or have disappeared. We don't even know if they really existed. It was the ancient Greeks who named the "Wonders" for their grand architecture or natural beauty. Have you heard of them? They are the Hanging Gardens of Babylon, the Temple of Artemis at Ephesus, the Mausoleum of Halicarnassus, the Colossus of Rhodes, the Statue of Zeus at Olympus, and the Lighthouse of Alexandria. It's a list that is more than 2,200 years old. But when you travel, you can make up your own list of wonders!

The Arts

**I served beauty.
Is there anything
greater in the world?"**

Sappho (end of 6th century–7th century B.C.E.)

Paintings, books, plays, sculptures, music, and films—works of art can be timeless. From prehistoric cave drawings and storytelling around the fire to digital art and blogs today, we've always wanted to share our vision and feelings about the world around us. The greatest works of art outlive their creators through their beauty and universal meaning.

Alonso Quixano read so much about knights that he wanted to be a knight too, and have his own adventures. In his attic, he found old armor, a dusty helmet, and a rusty sword, and that was all he needed to become Don Quixote de la Mancha and set off with his faithful servant, Sancho Panza, on the roads of Spain to conquer the world. This fictional hero of Miguel Cervantes fought windmills that he mistook for giants, and sheep that he thought were armies. But he never for a second doubted their reality! Is that because literature, in the words of Marcel Proust, "is the only life that's really lived?"

Stories on Paper

Words introduce us to our first heroes. A writer uses words to create characters that live in our imaginations each time we read their stories, often centuries after they were first written.

On his odyssey, the clever **Ulysses** escaped the Cyclops Polyphemus by blinding him.

The Greek poet **Homer** (8th century B.C.E.) composed the epic poems *The Iliad* and *The Odyssey*.

A Thousand and One Nights is a collection of ancient Arabic stories including *Ali Baba* and *Sinbad the Sailor*.

Ali Baba discovered the den of the forty thieves.

In his stories of knights, **Christian of Troyes** (12th century) introduced us to King Arthur, Lancelot, Percival, and the other Knights of the Round Table.

Against his mother's wishes, **Percival** decided to become a knight and pledge his faith to King Arthur.

In the 16th century, **François Rabelais** created the giant **Gargantua** and wrote clever stories about his adventures. One of them was about stealing the bells from a cathedral to put around his donkey's neck.

The Crow and the Fox

Poet **Jean de la Fontaine** (17th century) is best known for his animal fables, inspired by the ancient Greek storyteller Aesop.

The German **Brothers Grimm** (19th century) mine folklore and fairy tales for their famous story collections.

Little Red Riding Hood

184

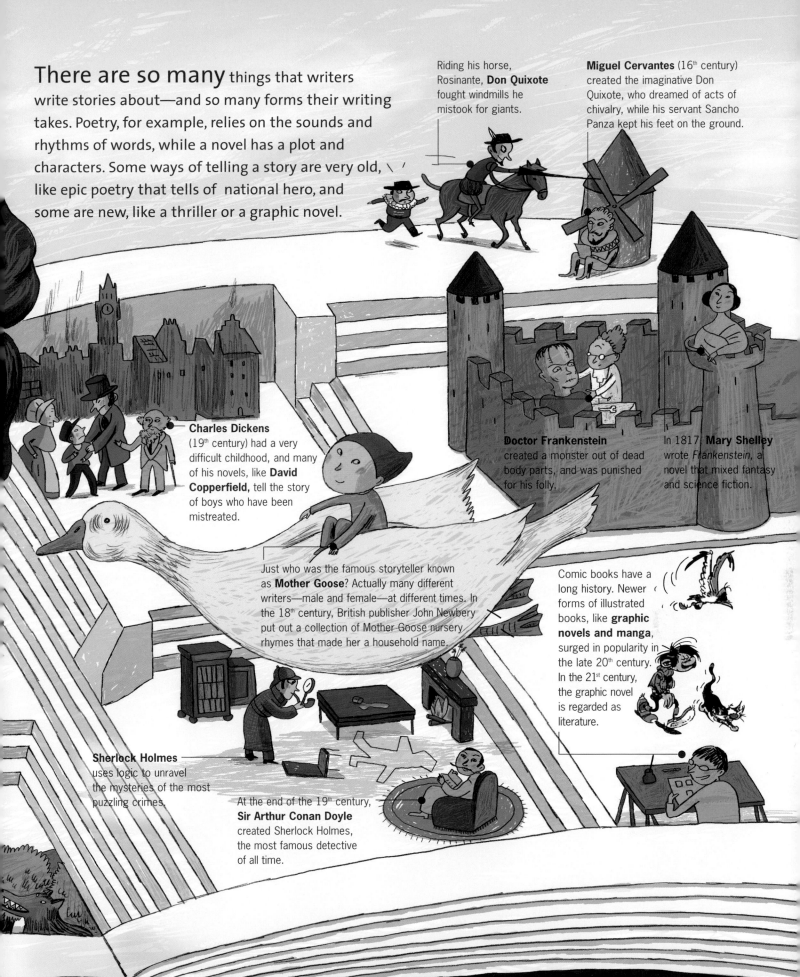

There are so many things that writers write stories about—and so many forms their writing takes. Poetry, for example, relies on the sounds and rhythms of words, while a novel has a plot and characters. Some ways of telling a story are very old, like epic poetry that tells of national hero, and some are new, like a thriller or a graphic novel.

Riding his horse, Rosinante, **Don Quixote** fought windmills he mistook for giants.

Miguel Cervantes (16th century) created the imaginative Don Quixote, who dreamed of acts of chivalry, while his servant Sancho Panza kept his feet on the ground.

Charles Dickens (19th century) had a very difficult childhood, and many of his novels, like **David Copperfield,** tell the story of boys who have been mistreated.

Doctor Frankenstein created a monster out of dead body parts, and was punished for his folly.

In 1817, **Mary Shelley** wrote *Frankenstein,* a novel that mixed fantasy and science fiction.

Just who was the famous storyteller known as **Mother Goose**? Actually many different writers—male and female—at different times. In the 18th century, British publisher John Newbery put out a collection of Mother Goose nursery rhymes that made her a household name.

Comic books have a long history. Newer forms of illustrated books, like **graphic novels and manga**, surged in popularity in the late 20th century. In the 21st century, the graphic novel is regarded as literature.

Sherlock Holmes uses logic to unravel the mysteries of the most puzzling crimes.

At the end of the 19th century, **Sir Arthur Conan Doyle** created Sherlock Holmes, the most famous detective of all time.

Quiet on the Set!

At the theater and in the movies, actors play roles. But theater is live, and things can change from one show to the next, while in movies one version is caught forever on film.

Every second of **animation** consists of 24 different drawings

Comedies try to make you laugh.

The **director** is in charge of the actors and technical people, and supervises the film's editing. Sometimes he or she also writes the story and the script.

The **cinematographer** shoots scenes with a camera.

Make-up keeps the actors looking good.

A **science fiction** movie tells of a future world run by technology.

Actors might have to do a scene 20 times before the director decides it is useable.

A **thriller** pits a detective against a criminal in a chase full of suspense.

A **Western** has horses and cowboys and adventure.

When scenes are dangerous, a **stuntman** or **stuntwoman** takes over from the starring actor.

A **boom operator** picks up the actors' voices.

The **key grip** puts down dolly tracks and moves the cameras.

A **gaffer** sets up the lights.

The **sound engineer** makes sure sound is recorded.

Continuity keeps track of everything in a scene so that things are where they need to be on each take.

Wardrobe is in charge of the costumes.

Movies are a combination of art, technology, and business. It's hard to believe that film was invented just a little more than 100 years ago! At first movies were in black and white and were silent, then sound was added (1927) and finally, color (1935). Today, special effects are so spectacular that the most fantastic worlds seem totally real.

Western theater was invented in ancient Greece around the 6th century B.C.E. with the first dramas: comedies and tragedies. Since then, theater has evolved constantly, but the great classics are still performed today, in new ways. In 2,500 years, theater has never stopped renewing itself.

In the 19th century, **Gilbert and Sullivan** perfected the comic operetta of songs and dance. The musical grew out of it.

Noh is Japanese theater from the 14th century. It deals with spiritual subjects using song, dance, masks, and mime.

HEATER

At each performance of a play, the **actors** keep polishing their lines and adding finishing touches to their parts. The audience is different every night, but the emotions of the story stay the same.

In the 20th century, **directors and playwrights** reinvented the theater. Eugene Ionesco, among others, created "Theater of the Absurd"—plays that didn't seem to follow any logic. Often they had a dreamlike mood.

In 16th century Italy, **Commedia dell'Arte** had stock characters like Harlequin and Pantalone. The stories were often improvised, so the actors had to be quick-witted.

William Shakespeare and **Christopher Marlowe** were great English playwrights of the 17th century. They both wrote historical dramas and poetry, but Shakespeare also wrote brilliant comedies. His plays are still widely enjoyed.

In India, actors wearing masks recount adventures of the gods and kings on stage in adaptations of epic poems like the **Ramayana** and the **Mahabharata.**

KNOW-IT-ALL NEWS

Vera Smart
Editor-in-chief

Ashley Asks
Interviewer

Tex A. Snap
Photo Journalist

Claire Itty
Researcher

Art Phul
Illustrator

Ed Shorter
News Briefs

From the Editor's Desk

Circuses can mean clowns, riders on horseback, elephants, and jugglers. But since the 1970s, there have also been theatrical circuses, focusing on one circus art like the trapeze or acrobatics.

Vera Smart

Art Phul

Welcome, Boys & Girls:
Under the Big Top!

The story of the circus begins in ancient Rome, where "circus" meant arena.

Today we have old-style acts with animals, and new-style shows based on theater.

Ashley Asks

Sam Falstaff is a wild animal trainer at the circus.

Sam, how do you train lions and tigers?

I watch their behavior very carefully and talk to them a lot, calling each one by name. They get used to the sound of my voice. I tell them when they're being good and I tell them when they're not. Before the 1930s, the usual training method was with force, using metal bars and choke collars. Fortunately trainers have changed!

Circus School

There are circus schools for grown-ups, but also ones for kids. Maybe there's one in your town where you can learn to walk a tightrope, twirl a plate on a stick, juggle three balls, and balance on a big balloon.

The Circus Is in Town!

Traditional circuses still travel from town to town. They put up posters, use loudspeakers to announce their arrival, and sometimes stage a parade. You can watch the Big Top go up before your eyes!

Ed Shorter

The **Cirque du Soleil** performs all over the world but it began in 1984 in Quebec, Canada. The company reinvented the circus from the ground up, using staging, costumes, acrobatics, choreography, and music to create stunning theatrical shows.

The circus is considered a family—and sometimes it really is. **The Flying Wallendas** trace their circus history back to the 17th century. But it was Karl Wallenda, born in Germany in 1905, who founded the family troupe that still performs today. He invented the seven-person chair pyramid balanced on top of the high wire. So many of Karl's grandchildren and great-grandchildren work in the circus today that they have split into several groups, including the Great Wallendas and the Fabulous Wallendas.

There were originally seven **Ringling Brothers** who started the circus that bears their name. In 1870, when it was known as The Ringling Brothers United Monster Shows, Great Double Circus, Royal European Menagerie, Museum, Caravan, and Congress of Trained Animals, it traveled by horse-drawn wagon and on foot from town to town. In 1889 they came up with the idea of putting the acts on a train and taking the circus all across America. Their competition was **Barnum and Bailey's**, which in 1882 was most famous for having Jumbo, the world's largest elephant. In 1919, the two circuses joined up and have been entertaining boys and girls of all ages with elephants, tigers, human cannonballs, and magnificent horses ever since.

Tex A. Snap

Cirque du Soleil is now made up of 2,500 people, including 500 artists of 40 different nationalities, and is the very definition of the modern circus: no animal acts, but lots of breathtaking dance, acrobatics, and clowns.

Do wild animals want to work?

Sometimes in rehearsals a tiger will leap up on his stool and lie down for a nap. You've got to keep encouraging them.

Does it take a lot to put together an act?

Yes! Months of rehearsals. I have to make them work every day so they know exactly when they are supposed to roll over or jump through a hoop. And I've got to feed them. Believe me, those big cats sure eat a lot of meat!

Are you ever afraid?

I never forget that they are wild animals. Even if they know me well, I always stay alert.

Giggles & Company:
**Fake Noses,
Giant Shoes,
Oversized Pants...**

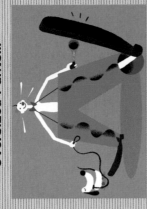

Everything a clown needs to be a pro!

So Much to See!

Artists—whether they're sculptors, painters, or photographers— aren't looking to simply copy what they see. They want to create an image that works with what they feel, and how they see the world.

Exhibition
THE CHILD
in Art

Welcome to the exhibition! How many children can you find in art here?

The **ancient Egyptians** believed that statues had life, like the people they represented. This is *The Dwarf Seneb and his Family*, painted limestone, from 2400 B.C.E.

In his *Madonna and the Goldfinch*, **Raphael** (1483–1520) gives his picture a feeling of depth by using the new skills of painting with perspective, developed in Italy during the Renaissance.

Diego Velasquez (1599–1660) was a court painter in Spain and often painted the eldest son of King Philip IV. Here the six-year-old is shown as a general.

Painting means applying colors taken from natural materials onto a surface, such as canvas, a rock, a wall, or paper. The pigments might be mixed with water to create a watercolor or a fresco, or with oil to create an oil painting. Artists today also use acrylic paint.

Sculpture consists of creating 3-dimensional forms in rock, clay, metal, or wood, using angles, hollows, shadows and light.

Photography was invented in the 19th century. It works by using light to capture an image on a sensitive surface, like paper. Today, art photographers use digital cameras and film cameras.

In *Maya and the Doll*, **Pablo Picasso** (1881–1973) challenged classical painting by showing the little girl's face from the front and in profile at the same time.

For a long time, art was tied to religion. Painted
or sculpted images were a link between people and the divine in
ancient Egypt, Africa, and Christian Europe in the Middle Ages. In the
Renaissance, art focused on the idea of beauty, but today
beauty is no longer agreed on as being the only purpose
of art.

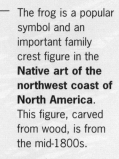

The frog is a popular symbol and an important family crest figure in the **Native art of the northwest coast of North America**. This figure, carved from wood, is from the mid-1800s.

A 12th century **Byzantine artist** painted the *Virgin of Vladimir*, an icon of the Virgin Mary and her son Jesus. The painter does not use perspective, so the picture looks flat.

Greek artists showed the human body perfectly proportioned. This terra cotta figurine (3rd century B.C.E.) shows Eros, the god of love, as a chubby little boy.

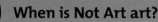

Impressionist artist **Auguste Renoir** (1841–1919) painted his canvas with bright colors and small brushstrokes to capture the feeling of lightness he saw in his subject. This is *Gabrielle and Jean*.

tune in...

When is Not Art art?

When it's Conceptual Art. Conceptual Art says that the entire process of making art is art itself. It started with the Dada movement in the early 20th century, when Marcel Duchamp displayed a bicycle wheel in 1913 and called it Bicycle Wheel. Two of the most successful conceptual artists are Christo and Jeanne-Claude who make installations in cities and landscapes. In 1991, they opened 3,100 umbrellas—yellow in California and blue in Ibaraki, Japan—and left them out for 19 days to be visited by the public.

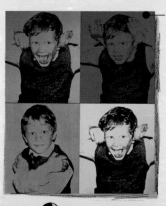

Andy Warhol (1928–1987) was one of the inventors of Pop Art. He used images of a consumer society, like cans of soup and Coke bottles, as well brightly tinted photographs of celebrities. This is *Magnus*, 1986.

The famous French photographer **Édouard Boubat** (1923–1999) captured scenes from daily life—the ordinary things that can become magical moments. Here, children are playing in Paris in 1953.

Music and Dance

On stage, the dancers are performing a **romantic ballet**: *Swan Lake* by Peter Tschaikovsky. Dancing on toe point began at the end of the 18th century.

You could call music the universal language of emotion. Whether it was written yesterday or three centuries ago, music never loses its beauty.

Kettle drums

Glockenspiel

Tuba

Bass drum

French horn

Harp

Bassoon

For centuries, if you wanted to hear music, you had to go to a concert. But **radio** (in the 1920s) and then **record albums** (in the 1940s) allowed anyone to listen anywhere.

Swan Lake

Viola

Violin

Cello

A **symphony orchestra** has more than 100 musicians divided into four sections: strings, brass, woods, and percussion.

The **conductor** interprets the music and leads his musicians to play together as a harmonized group.

Music is sounds combined in a certain rhythm. Noise—the wind, a jackhammer—isn't the same thing. Music must have an artistic intention. You can make music using your voice, or with instruments that have been invented over the centuries to make musical sounds when you pinch, rub, tap, hit, or blow. Dance, the art of movement in space, needs music, but music doesn't need dance.

Drums

Grand piano

Contrabass

Jazz was invented in the 1890s by black musicians in American cities like New Orleans and Chicago. Improvisation plays a big part in the music. *Jazz greats: Louis Armstrong, Miles Davis, John Coltrane.*

Saxophone

Hip-hop music, also known as **rap**, uses rhythmic lyrics and a strong beat. Breakdancing is the first dance that came out of hip-hop.

The voice is the first musical instrument. Choral singing blends different voices from high to low: soprano, alto, tenor, and bass.

Wolfgang Amadeus Mozart

Born: January 27, 1756.
Career: Musician and composer. **Childhood:** Brilliant young pianist and violinist. When Wolfgang was only seven, his father Leopold, a strict music teacher, took him on a concert tour of the courts of Europe. He wrote his first musical compositions at the age of five. **Works:** Operas, masses, symphonies, concertos, chamber music. He died in poverty at the age of thirty-five, leaving behind 700 works, including the opera *Don Giovanni* (1781), the *Jupiter* symphony (1788), and the *Requiem* (1791).

Violin

Contrabass

Bandoneón

Grand piano

Guitars

Drums

Bass

Rock and roll was born in the 1950s as a combination of African–American rhythm and blues, and country and western. *Great rockers: Elvis Presley, The Beatles, U2.*

The tango is music with a slow rhythm. It began in Argentina, and in 1912 was introduced to the world as a popular dance.

Indian classical dance is originally religious. It has very specific movements, including 67 hand gestures.

Sitar

Beginning in the late 1980s, **house** became popular as electronic dance music. It was a mixture of techno sounds, and remixes of other music.

Folk songs are the traditional music of a people. They have often been passed down through a community by word of mouth, and the songs usually tell a story.

Accordion

600	First **Gregorian chants**.
1721	**Johann Sebastien Bach** composes his Brandenburg Concertos.
1786	**Wolfgang Amadeus Mozart** writes the opera *The Marriage of Figaro*.
1810	**Ludwig van Beethoven** writes *The Emperor* piano concerto.
1882	**Richard Wagner** writes the opera *Parsifal*.
1913	**Igor Stravinski** creates a scandal with his ballet *The Rites of Spring*.
1925	Jazz trumpeter **Louis Armstrong** records *Cornet Chop Suey*.
1967	**The Beatles** release their album *Sgt. Pepper's Lonely Hearts Club Band*.
1978	Reggae singer **Bob Marley** brings out his album *Babylon by Bus*.
1983	Rappers **Run-D.M.C.** release their first single, *It's Like That*.

193

Art of the Builder

People build houses to live in them. But they also build buildings meant to last a long time—temples and churches to pray in, museums to display great art, palaces and castles meant to show off the power of kings and lords.

The pointed pediment, columns, and carvings of **Greek temples** inspired the Romans, and then, after the Renaissance, all of the West.

Houses in the Middle Ages were framed in wood. The spaces between the beams were packed with mud or bricks.

To bring water to towns 2,000 years ago, the **Romans** built aqueducts—they were bridges and tunnels that were slightly tilted to allow water to flow.

For the longest time, people

built mainly with stone, which was strong and easy to quarry, and wood. But starting in the 19th century, new materials like steel, glass, and concrete slowly replaced them. Building techniques also changed. The mechanical pulley systems of antiquity gave rise over thousands of years to today's contruction site—where huge cranes can put together a skyscraper in no time.

In the Middle Ages, **Romanesque churches** were shaped like a cross and had vaulted ceilings. The tympanum over the doors was often covered in sculpture.

tympanum

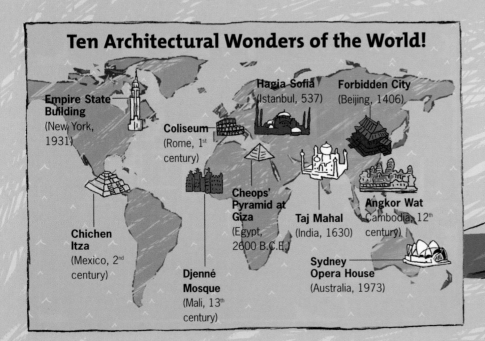

Ten Architectural Wonders of the World!

Empire State Building (New York, 1931)

Coliseum (Rome, 1st century)

Hagia Sofia (Istanbul, 537)

Forbidden City (Beijing, 1406)

Chichen Itza (Mexico, 2nd century)

Cheops' Pyramid at Giza (Egypt, 2600 B.C.E.)

Taj Mahal (India, 1630)

Angkor Wat (Cambodia, 12th century)

Djenné Mosque (Mali, 13th century)

Sydney Opera House (Australia, 1973)

In the Middle Ages, the lord lived in his **castle**. Everything about it was designed to withstand a siege, from its crenellated towers, to its ramparts and drawbridge.

Architect

An architect designs or re-designs a building. To see what form it should take, she must draw project plans using a computer, and decide what building materials would work best. She can't, for example, build a skyscraper out of bricks—it would crumble! Once the plan is accepted, she hires the builders and supervises the work on the construction site.

Starting in the 12th century in Europe, the **Gothic style** took over from the Roman. Churches became taller and lighter. They had stained glass windows.

During the 15th century, **Renaissance** style borrowed from classical Rome and Greece. Palaces featured columns and elegant gardens.

Some towns in Europe and the Middle East were protected by a **city wall** that kept other people out.

Without elevators, **skyscrapers** would be unthinkable! They were first built in the 19th century in the United States.

tained glass

City planning is the art of managing how spaces are used in a town. It was invented in the 19th century.

For centuries, bridges were built out of stone. When steel was invented in the 19th century, huge **suspension bridges** became possible.

In the 20th century, many apartment buildings and schools are built out of **concrete** on mechanized construction sites.

The railroad came to be during the Industrial Revolution of the 19th century. **Stations** built from metal sprouted up everywhere.

When a city wants to build a museum or a concert hall, **architects** are invited to submit plans to a competition where The best is chosen.

195

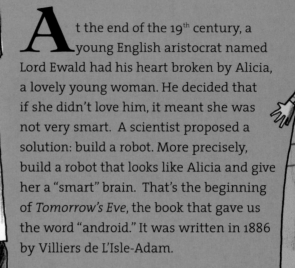

"
A scientist is not a person who gives the right answers; he is the one who asks the right questions."

Claude Lévi-Strauss (born 1908)

At the end of the 19th century, a young English aristocrat named Lord Ewald had his heart broken by Alicia, a lovely young woman. He decided that if she didn't love him, it meant she was not very smart. A scientist proposed a solution: build a robot. More precisely, build a robot that looks like Alicia and give her a "smart" brain. That's the beginning of *Tomorrow's Eve*, the book that gave us the word "android." It was written in 1886 by Villiers de L'Isle-Adam.

In a Greek myth, the Titan Prometheus wandered the Earth in search of living things. Not finding any, he made a human shape out of clay and rain water. Athena, goddess of wisdom, gave the shape a soul, and that is how the first person came to be. Prometheus made more humans, and acted as a proud father to them all. He taught them to read, to write, and to count. He taught them science and the arts. High on Mount Olympus, Zeus didn't like what he saw. He punished Prometheus brutally, but it was too late—the Titan had already given humans knowledge.

Science and Technology

All through the year 1999, people lived in fear of the Y2K (Year 2000) bug. It was widely believed that at the stroke of midnight, December 31, 1999, the whole world would break down. The way computers' internal clocks had been set, instead of going to 2000, they would go back to 1900. And all the things in the world that rely on accurate timing would grind to a halt: electricity would be cut off, elevators wouldn't work, subway cars would collide, airplanes would crash, and so on. Could we fix it all in time? But as midnight struck on December 31, 1999...everything went smoothly. It very quietly and calmly became the year 2000. The Y2K bug never happened despite all the advance hysteria.

Today's engineers and researchers face the same challenges as our earliest ancestors: to improve our lives, we need to invent, and we need to understand science and technology so we can take better care of ourselves and our planet. That's how dreams become reality and the impossible becomes the possible.

" There is no great genius without some touch of madness."

Lucius Annaeus Seneca (4 B.C.E.–65 C.E.)

Albert Robida spent the 19th century imagining what was to come. In his book, *The Twentieth Century*, written in 1883, he imagined record albums, the telephone, and the video recorder. But most importantly, he imagined the "telephonoscope," a gigantic crystal screen hanging on the wall of your living room that would pick up live broadcasts of shows, or allow you to have a conversation with someone on the other side of the planet. Imagine imagining the flat screen monitor before anyone had even thought of television or computers!

Inventors and Inventions

Without them we'd still be in the Stone Age. Inventors imagine and build extraordinary new things that have never been seen before. Some of their inventions have changed the way we live forever.

Water pours and turns wheels that make a floating object rise. The **clepsydra,** or **water clock,** keeps good time.

In a **pipe organ**, air is compressed by a pedal pump. The pipe sounds a note.

Like other machines that lift, a **crane** relies on gears.

A **flying machine** that imitates the flight of birds. But a man can't flap his arms fast enough, so this was an impossible dream.

A **steam engine** relies — on boiling water to move a piston that pushes a wheel

piston

Ctesibius about 300 B.C.E.

Archimedes discovered the screw and the lever. **Ctesibius** made ingenious machines with water and air.

An **odometer** measures distances. A pebble drops with each turn of the wheel—then you count the pebbles.

Da Vinci in 1485

Leonardo da Vinci was an artist, soldier, designer, and architect. He observed nature and used mathematics to invent new machines.

There's no magic formula to becoming an inventor. It takes a curious and original mind that is open to new ideas, and a willingness to take current ideas and bring them a step forward into the future. Or the ability to take an accident and turn it into something that works. It also takes a lot of hard work and determination to turn an idea into something real. Ctesibius and the Greek mechanics, da Vinci and the engineers of the Renaissance, Watt and the inventors of the Industrial Revolution, Edison and the entrepreneurs of the 19th century, Bardeen, Brattain, and Shockley and the researchers of the 20th century, all had something in common: they invented for the sheer joy of it.

Timeline

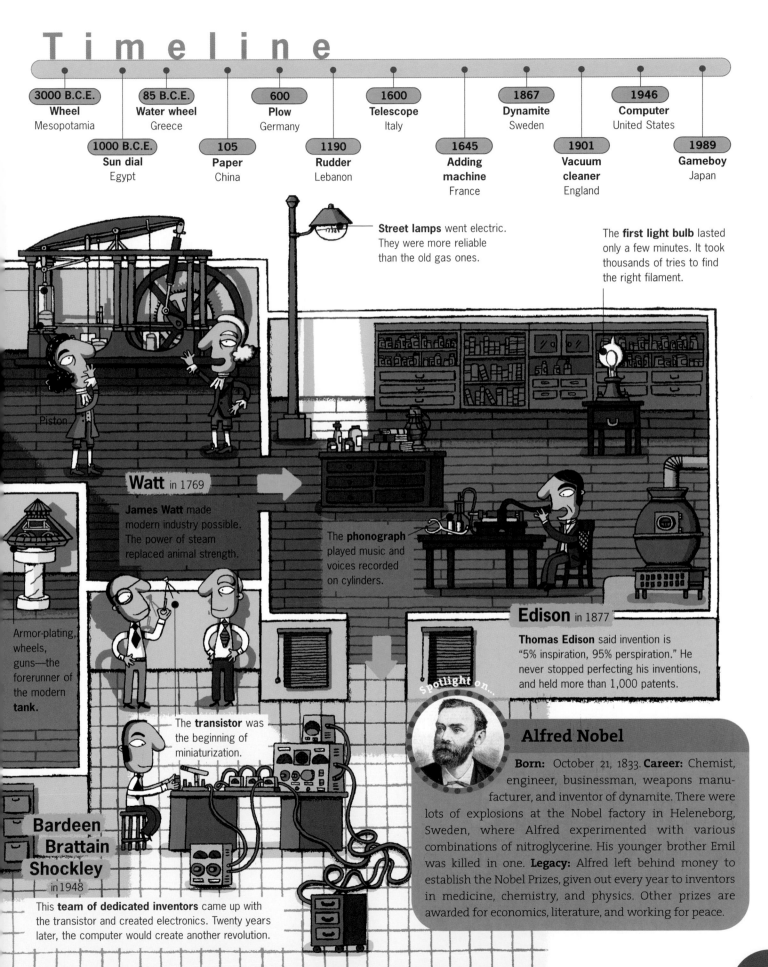

3000 B.C.E.		85 B.C.E.		600		1600		1867		1946
Wheel		**Water wheel**		**Plow**		**Telescope**		**Dynamite**		**Computer**
Mesopotamia		Greece		Germany		Italy		Sweden		United States

1000 B.C.E.		105		1190		1645		1901		1989
Sun dial		**Paper**		**Rudder**		**Adding machine**		**Vacuum cleaner**		**Gameboy**
Egypt		China		Lebanon		France		England		Japan

Street lamps went electric. They were more reliable than the old gas ones.

The **first light bulb** lasted only a few minutes. It took thousands of tries to find the right filament.

Piston

Watt in 1769

James Watt made modern industry possible. The power of steam replaced animal strength.

The **phonograph** played music and voices recorded on cylinders.

Armor-plating, wheels, guns—the forerunner of the modern **tank.**

Edison in 1877

Thomas Edison said invention is "5% inspiration, 95% perspiration." He never stopped perfecting his inventions, and held more than 1,000 patents.

The **transistor** was the beginning of miniaturization.

Bardeen Brattain Shockley in 1948

This **team of dedicated inventors** came up with the transistor and created electronics. Twenty years later, the computer would create another revolution.

Spotlight on...

Alfred Nobel

Born: October 21, 1833. **Career:** Chemist, engineer, businessman, weapons manufacturer, and inventor of dynamite. There were lots of explosions at the Nobel factory in Heleneborg, Sweden, where Alfred experimented with various combinations of nitroglycerine. His younger brother Emil was killed in one. **Legacy:** Alfred left behind money to establish the Nobel Prizes, given out every year to inventors in medicine, chemistry, and physics. Other prizes are awarded for economics, literature, and working for peace.

199

Faster! Farther!

It's hard to discover the world on foot or on horseback. Transportation has improved so much over the years that mountains and oceans are no longer obstacles, and the sky and space are new frontiers.

Stephenson's **Rocket**, 1829. 47 km (29 miles) per hour.

The **high speed train**— 1990, 500 km (311 miles) per hour—makes rail travel 10 times faster than it was 150 years ago.

Every means of transport has a forerunner.

And what amazing progress has been made between the first of something and its most recent incarnation! For a long time, wind and animal strength were the only sources of power. Then came the steam engine, and with it the train, and then the car and the plane. The combustion engine broke speed and distance records. Now, there are new engines being invented using different sources of energy that will take us far into space and to the bottom of the ocean.

Car by Karl Benz, Germany, 1894. 21 km (13 miles) per hour.

Handlebars, chain, pedals, brakes, and tires all had to be invented to go from the celeripede to the **mountain bike**.

Merlin's **rollerskate** (around 1700)

The **car of tomorrow** will have anti-collision radar, smart acceleration, and on-board computers that will adapt the ride to traffic and road conditions.

Celeripede 1791

Wheels have gone from wood to metal, and now plastic has turned skates into **rollerblades**.

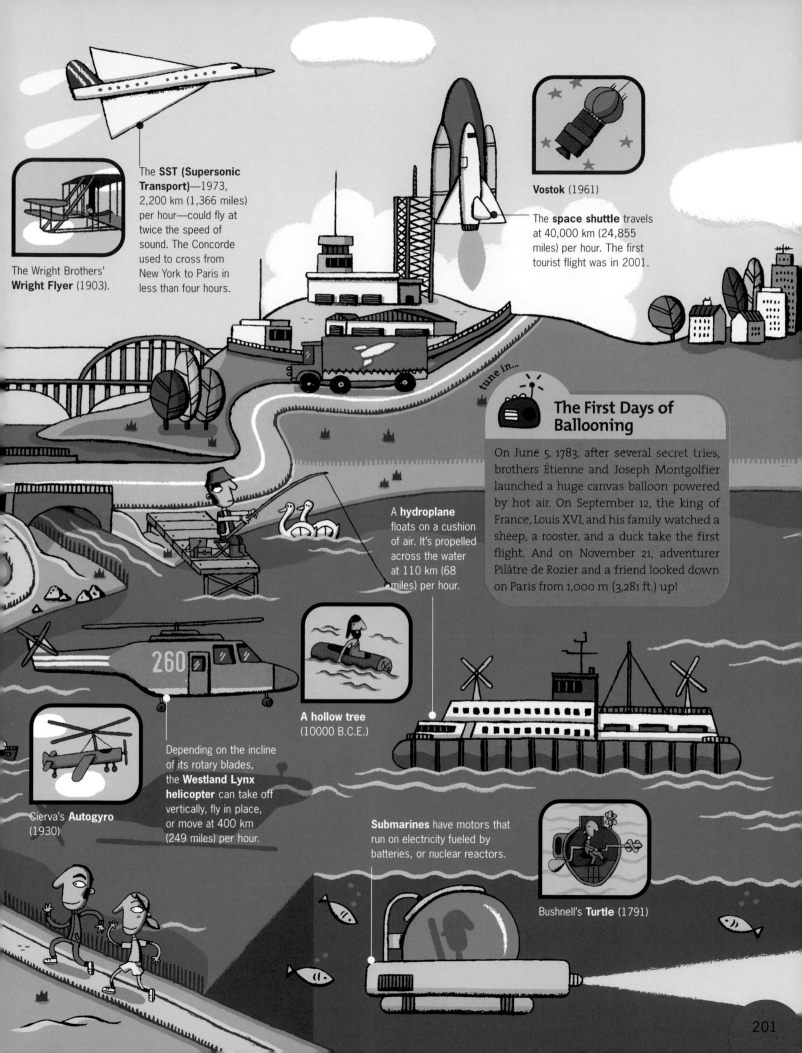

The **SST (Supersonic Transport)**—1973, 2,200 km (1,366 miles) per hour—could fly at twice the speed of sound. The Concorde used to cross from New York to Paris in less than four hours.

The Wright Brothers' **Wright Flyer** (1903).

Vostok (1961)

The **space shuttle** travels at 40,000 km (24,855 miles) per hour. The first tourist flight was in 2001.

A **hydroplane** floats on a cushion of air. It's propelled across the water at 110 km (68 miles) per hour.

tune in...

The First Days of Ballooning

On June 5, 1783, after several secret tries, brothers Étienne and Joseph Montgolfier launched a huge canvas balloon powered by hot air. On September 12, the king of France, Louis XVI, and his family watched a sheep, a rooster, and a duck take the first flight. And on November 21, adventurer Pilâtre de Rozier and a friend looked down on Paris from 1,000 m (3,281 ft.) up!

A hollow tree (10000 B.C.E.)

Depending on the incline of its rotary blades, the **Westland Lynx helicopter** can take off vertically, fly in place, or move at 400 km (249 miles) per hour.

Cierva's **Autogyro** (1930)

Submarines have motors that run on electricity fueled by batteries, or nuclear reactors.

Bushnell's **Turtle** (1791)

201

Solving the Mysteries of Daily Life

You plug in a gadget and push a button. Things light up. Or you hear noises. But how does it work? What's inside the case? Let's have a scientific look at the world we know.

A rushing ski run on the screen in your helmet, a downhill movement in your sensor boots—**virtual reality** is so *real!*

It used to be that everything was made out of natural materials like wood, leather, horn, or wool. Little by little, we learned to turn sand into glass, minerals into metals, and oil into plastics. Things became lighter, more practical, and cheaper. Now many materials are new inventions perfectly suited to their uses.

The fibers of this **polar fleece sweater** are made of recycled plastic bottles.

The colors you see on the **TV screen** are a combination of green, red, and blue light.

Yarn treated with tiny particles of **bamboo charcoal** give you socks with no sweating and no bad odor!

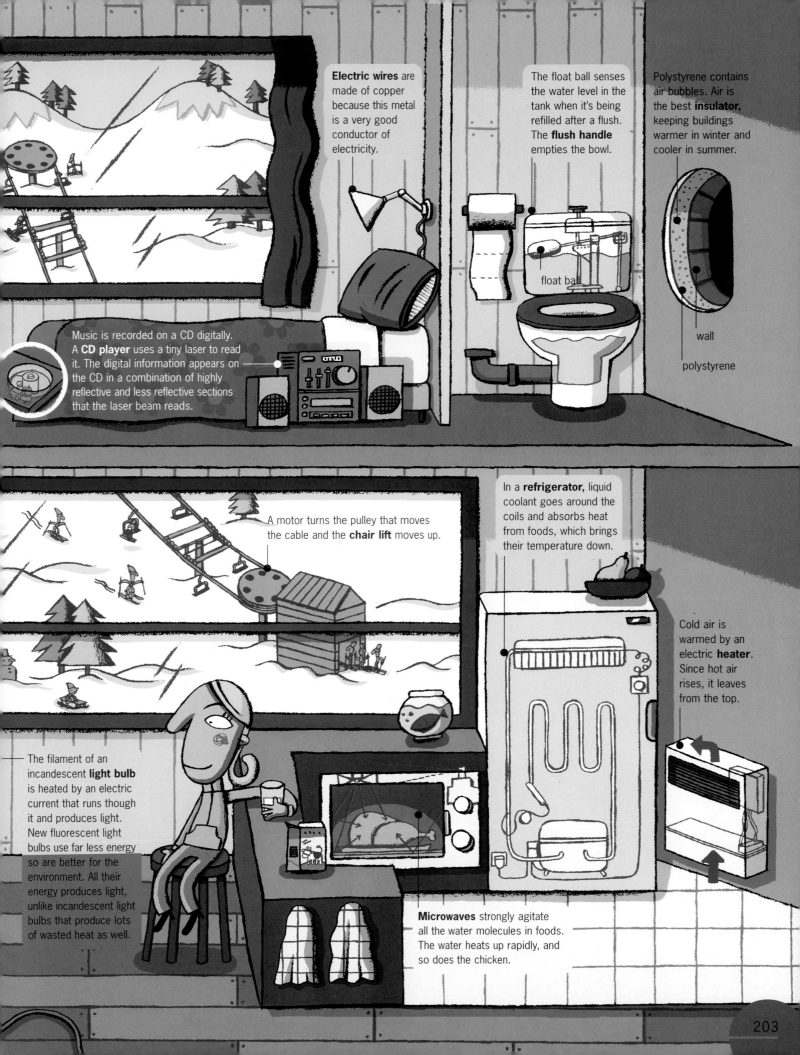

Electric wires are made of copper because this metal is a very good conductor of electricity.

The float ball senses the water level in the tank when it's being refilled after a flush. The **flush handle** empties the bowl.

Polystyrene contains air bubbles. Air is the best **insulator,** keeping buildings warmer in winter and cooler in summer.

float ball

wall

polystyrene

Music is recorded on a CD digitally. A **CD player** uses a tiny laser to read it. The digital information appears on the CD in a combination of highly reflective and less reflective sections that the laser beam reads.

A motor turns the pulley that moves the cable and the **chair lift** moves up.

In a **refrigerator,** liquid coolant goes around the coils and absorbs heat from foods, which brings their temperature down.

Cold air is warmed by an electric **heater**. Since hot air rises, it leaves from the top.

The filament of an incandescent **light bulb** is heated by an electric current that runs though it and produces light. New fluorescent light bulbs use far less energy so are better for the environment. All their energy produces light, unlike incandescent light bulbs that produce lots of wasted heat as well.

Microwaves strongly agitate all the water molecules in foods. The water heats up rapidly, and so does the chicken.

203

Out in Cyberspace

In our world, it's possible to know whatever, whenever. Thanks to networks of computer servers, you can chat, work, and play anywhere. We call this vast universe of information cyberspace.

MOVIES

Some **movies** feature characters and special effects created completely with computers.

CYBERCAFE

The more computers are connected, the more you can do on them. Email, websites, and blogs are all on the **World Wide Web.**

A **mobile phone** sends a signal to a computer that decides the best route for the call to travel.

Sound waves get weak over long distances. That's why there are **relays** to amplify sound between callers.

Wireless Application Protocol (WAP) allows phones to talk to computers.

You can now read **newspapers and magazines** in either a paper or electronic form.

Land lines require never-ending underground cables.

With an **MP3 player,** your music goes everywhere you go.

The information and communication revolution was made possible by digitization. By turning text, images, and sound into numbers, information can be stored, copied, sent, and shared. It's the biggest advance for spreading information since the printing press was invented more than 500 years ago.

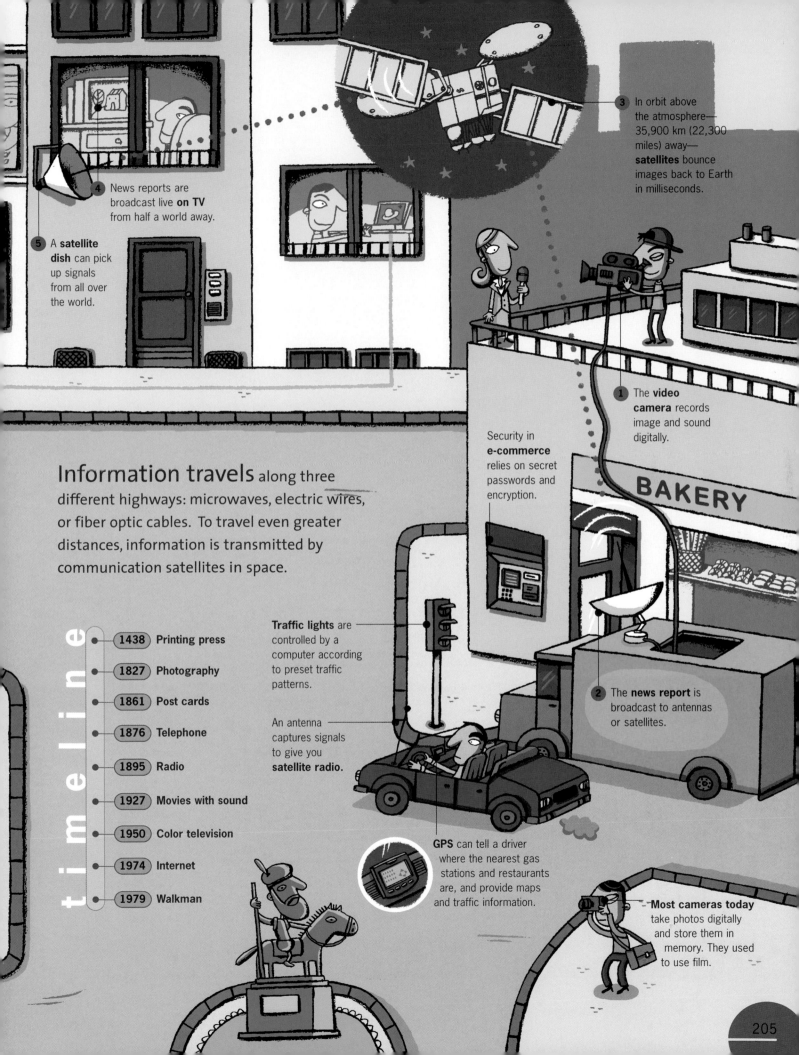

4 News reports are broadcast live **on TV** from half a world away.

5 A **satellite dish** can pick up signals from all over the world.

3 In orbit above the atmosphere—35,900 km (22,300 miles) away—**satellites** bounce images back to Earth in milliseconds.

Security in **e-commerce** relies on secret passwords and encryption.

1 The **video camera** records image and sound digitally.

BAKERY

Information travels along three different highways: microwaves, electric wires, or fiber optic cables. To travel even greater distances, information is transmitted by communication satellites in space.

2 The **news report** is broadcast to antennas or satellites.

Traffic lights are controlled by a computer according to preset traffic patterns.

An antenna captures signals to give you **satellite radio.**

timeline

1438	Printing press
1827	Photography
1861	Post cards
1876	Telephone
1895	Radio
1927	Movies with sound
1950	Color television
1974	Internet
1979	Walkman

GPS can tell a driver where the nearest gas stations and restaurants are, and provide maps and traffic information.

Most cameras today take photos digitally and store them in memory. They used to use film.

Machines That Work

In a factory, things are designed and made with the help of computers. These powerful machines can receive, save, change, and transmit data. Computers can be used to make models, they control industrial robots, and they keep track of deliveries.

Welcome to our factory.

This is where we build cars.

For a car manufacturer, launching a new model is quite a feat. It takes almost two years to figure out everything customers will look for in a new car. Then the car company produces thousands of these new cars, sometimes in just one week. Virtual models, simulated crash tests, simulated weather conditions, and production robots make every minute count. It would be impossible without computers.

Inside the offices, new plans are kept secret. The designers are making a new model, known for now as X89. It's not easy to know what drivers will want! Possible customers are polled, and hundreds of **drawings** and **models** are made. Finally, the look of the X89 is set.

Here, they are building a prototype, or the first ever X89. Everything's got to be worked out—the exact dimensions, the materials, the colors of all the different parts—from the engine to the turn signal. The production machines and robots need to be tested now, too.

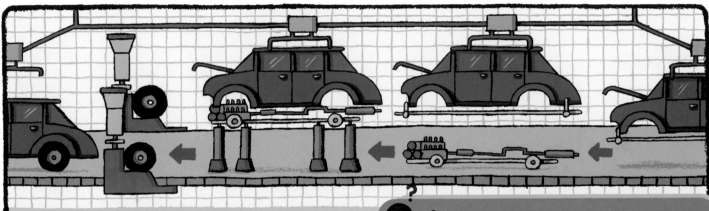

Here we are on the workshop floor. Everything is automated and perfectly synchronized, from welding the roof to adding on the doors to painting the body. The **central computer** controls the movements of robot welders, carriers, and painters. It's like conducting an orchestra.

This is the end of the assembly line. Here the dashboard panels, the engine, and the wheels are added. The important thing is to never run out of pieces. A **computer** keeps track of stock and orders parts as they are needed.

Are robots intelligent?

The only intelligence robots have is the one they are programmed with. Industrial robots can "see" with cameras and "touch" with their claws equipped with sensors. But they can't actually do anything on their own—they can only follow the computer's instructions. Robots that are made to be played with sometimes seem more clever because they "disobey." Unlike industrial robots, toy robots aren't programmed to make the same movements all the time, but to react to what's going on around them.

Once the final tuning is done, all the options—like color or sliding roof—are checked. There is never a mistake because each car has a **microchip** with everything the customer ordered written on it.

KNOW-IT-ALL NEWS

Vera Smart
Editor-in-chief

Ashley Asks
Interviewer

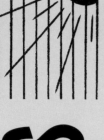

Tex A. Snap
Photo Journalist

Claire Itty
Researcher

Art Phul
Illustrator

Ed Shorter
News Briefs

From the Editor's Desk

For centuries, people have tried to make intelligent machines that seem alive—like an animal or person. At the end of the 20th century, new "smart" robots made for some really amazing toys.

Vera Smart

AIBO: The Robot as Family Pet!

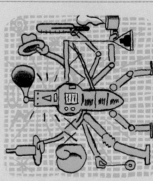

In 1999, Sony invented AIBO, a computer with paws and artificial intelligence. It had a program made up of four instincts (affection, curiosity, movement, and appetite) and six emotions (happiness, anger, sadness, surprise, fear, and discontent). Since 1999, newer and more perfected versions of an "intelligent companion" have been made. But today, Sony uses the AIBO technologies on other forms of electronic robots.

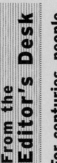

Art Phul

Ashley Asks

Akira Oshima has been collecting robots for more than 20 years.

Mr. Oshima, where does your passion for robots come from?
Maybe my first mechanical toys, or even the story of Pinocchio. I've always been amazed at machines that look a bit like us.

What is your oldest robot?
Eric, the first robot. He goes back to 1922, and was built for a play by Karel Capek. That's the author who invented the word "robot," which is based on the Czech word for work. That robot is radio controlled.

And the others?

I've restored automatons from the olden days. They were beautiful dolls that would play the piano, write, or speak. I'd love to find the famous chessplayer from 1750—people were sure there was a person hidden inside.

But do you really have robot servants?

They're more recent, dating back to the 1970s. They are programmed to cut the grass, polish the floor, cook, and water plants. They are stuffed with electronics. They are very odd computers.

What will happen in the next 20 years?

With the advances we're making in artificial intelligence, the next generation of robots will live with us, and take care of our needs. They'll be real companions.

Victor
The Car Robot
Keeps you awake at the wheel!

He rolls down windows!
He tells jokes!
He even sprays!

It also learns to recognize the question, "What is it?" When you show it the red ball and ask the question, the robot dog barks, "Ball!"

And if it sees a cherry for the first time, it makes a mistake because cherries, too, are round and red. Then you can teach it the word "cherry" and whatever else you want.

Tex A. Snap

AIBO learns to speak: researchers at Sony worked on a prototype that would recognize and name objects. The principle is simple: AIBO associates a red ball and the sound "ball."

News Briefs

Robo Cup The idea is to create robot soccer players that in 2050 can beat humans in the World Cup. There are matches held every year to guage the progress of this attempt at creating artificial intelligence. Already the robots communicate with each other, and remember their best moves.

Watch Your Step!

Many robots have been designed to imitate human behavior. Now there are some that can go up a staircase. It's a real technological feat because on each step the robot has to balance and figure out where to put its feet.

Ed Shorter

INDEX

PHOTOGRAPHY CREDITS